Fait

A Book That Will Help You Fight and Win A Life of Faith.

Pastor Howard A. Strickland

Faith that Wins

Copyright 2011 Dr. Howard A. Strickland

ISBN-13: 978-1456541880

Published by

New Psalm Publishing.com

$12.99

Acknowledgments

Faith is the answer, however, many times people make it too complicated. Pastor Strickland breaks faith down with a good owners manual to follow.

The pages in this book offer real help with your walk with God. Pastor Howard offers personal testimonies along with good theology mixed with humor for daily living.

Throughout this journey of life believers go through their up's and down's. Thankfully there is a way to endure the mundane, and difficult days, weeks and sometimes seasons.

The road less traveled is a sure and stable road of faith. Sometimes the journey of faith doesn't seem too feasible, and it seems just too hard; however, it offers eternal reward with powerful perks, even on this earth.

This book will offer real life solutions, along with sensible information that will stir faith, success, favor, gifts and love. You will even laugh at the humor of God at times.

Right off, as you read, you will experience God's blessings through practical facts and knowledge mixed with faith that's obtainable. This book is a keeper for any personal library.

Thank you to my lovely wife Jenny, you're my best friend and the love of my life. To my two boys, Nathan and Daniel, I thank God for you daily. Also to Crane Eater Community Church for all the inspiration I receive from you- it's infectious.

I would also like to thank the Church of God for its great leadership!

Bible Translations

Why use different translations and paraphrases?

For two reasons. First, the Bible was originally written using 11,280 Hebrew, Aramaic, and Greek words, but the typical English translation uses only around 6,000 words. Obviously, variation,and shades of meaning can be missed, so it is always helpful to compare translations.

Second, we often miss the full impact of familiar Bible verses, not because of poor translating, but simply because they have become so familiar. We think we know what a verse says because we have read it or heard it so many times. Then when we find it quoted in a book, we skim over it and miss the full meaning. Therefore I have deliberately used paraphrases in order to help you see God's truth in new, fresh ways.

What People are saying...

Doctor Raymond F. Culpepper...
General Overseer Church of God, Cleveland, Tennessee

Pastor Strickland interweaves personal stories from his own rich background of pastoral experiences. The remarkable trait of the telling of these true-life stories in the positive and uplifting manner in which they are told. Strickland establishes the Word as the absolute authority for confronting every single challenge of life.

This book isn't for one seeking misery, discouragement, or bitterness because of the conditions of the world or the attacks of the enemy.

Another characteristic of the book is the "down-to-earth" manner in which it is written. Neither clergy nor laity will find the material difficult to comprehend. But. at the same time the book also has a quality that leaves the reader with a feeling of assurance that the author "knows that of which he speaks."

This book will be both enjoyable and helpful to a wide range of Christian readers.

I proudly endorse this book!

Doctor Michael Baker...

Currently serves as the Administrative Bishop for North Georgia Church of God.

This book is about faith and winning! Fused with personal life experiences and scriptural insight, Pastor Strickland offers real life solutions that vividly paint scenes of faith and how Christ brings a winning formula to every person. It's about living faith, speaking faith and doing faith —it's about life's journey and understanding the power of faith to win. Read it and be encouraged, read it again and be strengthened. This book exudes faith. It's a winner!

Doctor Joe E. Edwards...

Senior Pastor of Church of Liberty Square in Cartersville, Georgia- a major ministry in Georgia of over 2,500 members.

Howard Strickland has written another inspiring and faith building book. One of the things that make his books effective is the fact he lives what he writes.

This book describes how one can live in a world that is rapidly changing and yet experience peace. The humor with which he communicates is very helpful. The illustrations come out of his personal experience and make the truths of this book real. Any minister will enjoy and glean much for use in ministering to his people."

Contents

INTRODUCTION

Through out God's word the reader will find story after story of men and women who braved through, and won the life of faith. However, many failed but they didn't give up.

Winning isn't easy, nor is it glamourous. Sometimes the up's and down's are more than many believers can take. Some throw-in the towel, and just decide to get by, or become average. It's important to mention though that any other lifestyle is always secondary.

If believer's can learn to win and remain stable no matter what he or she goes through they will excel and grow spiritually.

This book is based upon true life stories throughout God's word. Many of the central text used by Strickland will help the reader relate and understand that he or she is no different than those throughout scripture. However, these stories and key verses that stir up faith, along with Strickland's personal testimonies will bring new life, fire and hope unto every believer.

Chapter 1

The Life of A Winner - Faith

Faith is the confidence that what we hope for will actually happen; it gives us assurance about things we cannot see.

Through their faith, the people in days of old earned a good reputation. Women received their loved ones back again from death. But others were tortured, refusing to turn from God in order to be set free.

They placed their hope in a better life after the resurrection. Some were jeered at, and their backs were cut open with whips. Others were chained in prisons. Some died by stoning, some were sawed in half, and others were killed with the sword. Some went about wearing skins of sheep and goats, destitute and oppressed and mistreated.

They were too good for this world, wandering over deserts and mountains, hiding in caves and holes in the ground.

All these people earned a good reputation because of their faith, yet none of them received all that God had promised.

For God had something better in mind for us, so that they would not reach perfection without us.
Hebrews 11: 1-2, 35-40 NLT

Whatever people may tell you the highest level of faith is a faith that endures; a faith that confesses God's promises without seeing them.

Some will say, *"Oh the faith life is a life of ease,"* but nothing could be farther from the truth. Many begin their journey only to allow set backs to throw them off course. While others fall off the wagon, those who take the stand *"I shall not be moved"* and keep a pure spirit will experience God's best over the long haul. Remember, whatever you face today, it's not worthy to compare to the eternal.

What is a winning faith? Faith that wins is a real faith, a faith that pleases God, a faith that lasts. Winning faith changes the world one person at a time. Real faith hears, believes and does.

The 11th chapter of Hebrews is a moving account of faithful Old Testament saints. Many times our excuse is, *"well that's then, but I live in the twenty first century."* Remember, these saints didn't walk around with the living spirit of God dwelling inside as we do. *Do you not know that you are the temple of God and that the Spirit of God dwells in you?¹* No, but these men and women chose to take the limits off, and live life unchained. They walked and talked with the knowledge they knew, and became a powerful force to be reckoned with.

Always remember, the grace of God will take you where you are today and propel you into your future. Today as then, grace and faith work hand and hand.

The greatest point to be made about Christianity is, right now you can decide to excel, trust and believe. God will honor that, and right now you can begin a fresh faith future. F.F.F.

"Right now you can begin a fresh faith future. F.F.F."

Hebrews chapter eleven has been given the title "Heroes of faith." These men and women all attest to the value of living by faith. These faith heroes now compose of 'the cloud of witnesses' written of in Hebrews twelve. They gave great testimony to the non-believing Hebrews that they too should come into this dynamite faith and trust in the truth and authority of the ever-living gospel of God's word.

I think it's safe to say, these men and women had faith with muscles. They believed without much proof, they had a faith that went far beyond words; their faith was worthy to live, and even die for. These heroes had solid assurance that their future was better than their past, and this kept them going.

Let me remind you, this life will throw you a curve many times, but it isn't worthy to compare to your heavenly home. One man said, *"Earth is a long goodbye, while heaven is a long hello.*

The temporal, with all its trials, temptations, afflictions and setbacks seem to rub us the wrong way with bitter emotions that linger. Plus these trails try to settle our future.

For that very reason, I believe Hebrews eleven, begins by saying, *"Now faith is."* *Regardless what* you think right this very minute, faith is now. You can kneel now, hear from Jesus now, and believe now, change now and even receive anything by faith right now. However, if you chose to live without the reality of Christ, you won't be able to declare faith moment by moment. Again what you need is now faith. Now faith doesn't wait for favorable signs, or for the right people to get on board.

"Please remember, the only thing you can control is the now, and it's handled by your faith in God."

So what is faith? *Faith is Christ and He alone.* Let me explain, God's word declares, *in the beginning was the Word, and the Word was with God, and the Word was God. He was in the beginning with God. All things were made through Him, and without Him nothing was made that was made.*² When you speak God's word over your situations, problems or just life in general, you are speaking Christ, and He's the sword of the word of God. He will get it done. You might need a breakthrough right this moment, so speak the word, or should I say once again, *"speak Christ."*

"Fear, terror or dread can keep you up all night long, but faith makes one soft pillow."

Heaven is forever, so keep your priorities straight. What's actually important? If you aren't careful the mundane of the daily grind will throw you a curve and get you off course. How did the saints of old receive divine approval from God?

Listen, to Paul's words, *so we don't look at the troubles we can see now; rather, we fix our gaze on things that cannot be seen. For the things we see now will soon be gone, but the things we cannot see will last forever.*[3]

These elders had the ability to look beyond the physical into the spiritual; beyond the present to the future, and beyond the visible to the invisible. Simply put, they believed God and spoke with shadows and types of Christ. Knowing their Messiah was coming very soon. Think about it, living and speaking Christ without any proof. You say, *"I don't have proof,"* but oh my friend you do, *"it's in the sixty-six books of God's word."*

These elders of old obtained a favorable testimony because they quickly learned that faith is a journey. A person of faith never stops growing or learning.

It's been proven that those who continue to read keep their mind active, and these individuals live with a brighter healthier attitude. They learn through their own setbacks as well as the mistakes of others they read about. In their journey they learn to live humble while becoming a person of prayer. They submit their steps and even their thoughts before God. They lived submitted, submitted to the King of Kings and Lord of Lord's.

We need faith for living far more than for dying. Dying is easy work compared with living. Dying is a moment's transition; living a transition that takes years. Choose life and live! Glorify God in your life by being a lIVING sacrifice.

Every time the devil attacks you, he runs the risk of promoting and increasing you. The more the children of Israel were afflicted, the more they grew and multiplied. What doesn't kill you makes you stronger. Keep growing.[4]

The Bible declares, *These all died in faith, not having received the promises, but having seen them afar off were assured of them, embraced them and confessed that they were* strangers and pilgrims on the earth. For those who say such things declare plainly that they seek a homeland.[5]

This journey with God will help you through the dry times, through sorrow, pain and even loss. On this journey, our lives aren't lived as our own, or as robots, on the contrary, the decisions others make affect our movement; therefore, God intervenes. Everything God does is well timed, so run or walk onward my friend- walk on.

You who desire to go a thousand miles through faith, beyond what you have ever gone before, leap into it. Believe that the blood of Christ makes you clean; believe that you have come into resurrection life. Believe it! Trying is an effort, whereas believing is a fact. Don't join the Endeavor Society, but come into the Faith Society, and you will leap into the promises of God, which are "Yes" and "Amen" to all who believe.[6]

Author Brian Tracy was at a conference when he met Kop Kopmeyer, an expert in the field of success who has written four best sellers based on 250 principles he observed from fifty years of research. Tracy asked him, "Of the 1,000 success principles you

discovered, what's the most important?"
Without hesitation Kopmeyer replied, "Do
what you should do, when you should do it,
whether you feel like it or not.[7] Listen my
friend, that's faith talk mixed with action, and
that is exactly what these Old Testament saints
did, so we should do no less. John Mason once
said, *"It's not what we have but what we use,*
not what we see but what we choose- these
are the things that mar or bless human
happiness. Again, when you limit what you
will do, you limit what you can do."

"Do what you should do, when you should do it, whether you feel like it or not."

Doing faith doesn't stop; doing faith finishes
and completes the mission. These elders
weren't perfect, but they stayed faithful, and
even when they got off course they looked up
again and found their help.

Sometimes we have the tendency to think
these people were extra ordinary; however,

they were a people who faced difficult trails and conditions just as you and I do.

You can experience a good report as you go forward. Let no one fool you, faith is hard, slow and seemingly non-spiritual at *times*.

Women received their loved ones back from the dead. There was those who, under torture, refused to give in and go free, preferring something better: resurrection.[8] Wow, people being raised from the dead. Sounds exciting; however, remember life goes on; moreover, those raised didn't go on radio or television, no, they didn't write a book, or sell their story for a lump sum of money. They stayed fixed on the fact that Jesus Christ was raised from the dead, and one day, by faith, they would be raised too. Sure they were elated; however, again they kept their eyes on the promise- the resurrection.

Those who were tortured, they would not give in to anyone's agenda or theories. They refused to throw in the towel, they were better than that; moreover, you are too. Don't settle for seconds, God didn't.

There are many means of torture, just to name a few, nettles driven under the finger nails, slow burns under the arm pit, cutting the tongue off bit by bit, nails driven in, and through places I won't mention. Enough said; however, sometimes, the worse treatment is just being lonely, hungry for a touch, many live in pitch darkness, the screams of a spouse being tortured, or maybe children you know going down the wrong road in life.

Of course I made these up just to prove a fact. Anyone can come up with excuses because of life, and the blows we all take, but it takes a God fearing person to finish faith!

These heroes of faith are rewarded and rightfully so. Every person listed in Hebrews eleven went through difficult times, and even deadly events, and many suffered their own painful death.

Others braved abuse and whips, and, yes, chains and dungeons. We have stories of those who were stoned, sawed in two, murdered in cold blood; stories of vagrants wandering the earth in animal skins, homeless, friendless, powerless—the world didn't deserve them! — Making their way as best they could on the cruel edges of the world.[9] Need I say more? One thought, notice the ending of these verses, the world didn't deserve them.

Friend whatever you face in life, if you can just remember, *"Hey, the world doesn't deserve me, I'm heaven bound."* They bore their way through regardless.

Not one of these people, even though their lives of faith were exemplary, got their hands on what was promised. God had a better plan for them one day, their faith and, our faith would come together to make one completed whole, their lives of faith not complete apart from ours.[10] There you have it, at the end of this life, you will be made whole.

Remember, while some are getting Botox and Face-lifts trying to keep their decaying flesh looking pretty, or handsome one more year, you my friend of faith will receive a powerful forceful faith-lift into eternity one day.

Faith isn't for the halfhearted or quitters, it's for those who have knowledge and believe that God and His kingdom are worth it all.

Here are a few final thoughts about faith. First, **it's a journey.** Play hard and play to win, but remember, when the dust settles hard times will still occur. Companies as well as churches alike grow where there is passion, so live, work, and play with fervor. The cool part about being a believer is, our journey just begins upon our final grasp of breath.

Second, **Faith is a test.** One man told me a long time ago, don't allow your highs to be too high, and your lows, too low. Tests will come and go.

Back in 1990, as a young believer I watched a miracle transpire right before my eyes. Yes, it was a well-known speaker and author preaching in a local church.

A young girl was sitting beside me, along with her parents; the renowned speaker came off the platform and came toward this young girl to pray. She looked about twelve years of age. The speaker notices this young girl's fingers. Each finger twisted almost as though she had the fingers of someone a hundred years of age.

As the speaker prayed softly not once, twice, but seven times, and on the seventh prayer I watched with my own eyes (yes, I had my eyes open) as her fingers came into joint.

The mother and father begin crying, hugging, and thanking the Lord. I was too. Moreover, I will never forget that great evening when a little girl's physical appearance changed. This event left an impact on me because, nothing was done with hype, it was a miracle, and I experienced it first hand.

A wonderful thing happened sometime later; I saw this same evangelist again, so I asked him if he remember being at this certain church, and he said he remembered. So then I proceeded to ask him about this young girl, and the miracle that occurred through his ministry that particular night. He looked me square in my eyes and said, "I don't remember." I knew he remembered; however, to him it wasn't important, because he knew 'WHO' really deserved all the praise and glory.

He is a true man of faith, and would not dare try and share God's praise and glory.

You see my friend, "*if you take the praise in the good times, you will take the praise in the bad times, and that will always spell disaster.*"

Third, your faith will increase and grow. As it does, make sure you stay submitted and humble. I have seen men and women change, and actually think they've arrived without any help. At least, that's what many of them acted like. Remember, pride always comes before a fall. The things they once believed in, now they fuss over, and even complain that they could have done it better, or could have done it without their cohorts help. Listen, God won't bless self, or selfish gain.

Unlike Hebrews chapter eleven, I think it's important to mention, those the world classifies as stars and sports hero's, many of them refuse to allow their children to watch the very television programs they promoted, endorse, and receive royalties and pensions from.

Many of the rich, and famous refuse huge gifts around Christmas or birthdays for themselves, their spouses, or children because they understand what this lifestyle really promotes. The things they appear to stand for are very hypocritical and foolish compared to their own true beliefs.

Just a few weeks ago I heard one star say, "Oh no I would never allow my children to watch one of my films." They were ashamed of their own work in Hollywood.

So what I'm trying to point out is, "Don't believe everything you hear or see on television, or in a magazine it might be laughed at by the very ones who endorse that lifestyle or product."

Remember these heroes of faith in Hebrews eleven died without any worldly recognition. They knew their compensation would be waiting on the other side. But of course sowing and reaping does pay dividends because these men and women are forever named in God's eternal word.

Finally, faith produces fruit and gifts, plus it reproduces. Faith is infectious. Faith doesn't live alone, faith helps others, and it blooms while producing love, peace and gifts. Gifts that reach out, fruit that helps others grow, and in return that person becomes a powerful force for Jesus Christ.

Our denomination began in the hills of North Carolina, with just a handful of people that hungered for spiritual fullness. Once a year our church offers an opportunity for every believer new and old to go back in time, and revisit those humble beginnings. Every person can see first-hand where the Church of God began its roots. There's not much there, but some huge trees on a back road seemingly to nowhere. However, this is where a few saints of God gathered who knew He could carry them farther and give them more. You will find a small creek that once fed an old mill, probably used to grind corn, also a stone was placed there representing the modest point. Inscribed on the stone is, *Church of God founded in 1886.*

It never fails, as I'm standing there, I think of those who were severely persecuted for their faith. For stepping out and desiring more, jeopardizing their family and friends, while leaving the familiar. I weep, you know, a good gut-wrenching cry; I weep thinking of our large churches, as well as our smaller churches, with great men and women of God as pastors, with hungry congregations.

This kind of faith, many can, and will easily take for granted, but not me. Again, most of the true pioneers of faith paid a hefty price for their faith that has enhanced ours. My question to you is, "Does you faith enhance others?"

The sign reads, *"Church of God founded in 1886"*

Back in May of 1991, one fall afternoon I had a call that my church treasurer had been shot, so I rushed to the hospital to comfort his family. Upon arrival I found his wife and children around his bed with my friend in pain but smiling.

Come to find out, a young man rushed into a factory with a loaded gun, and began firing. He was very angry and jealous over his girl friend breaking up with him, so he proceeded to shoot anyone who came in contact with him.

This was my first pastorate and tithes were few.

My friend's testimony was always the same; *"I will place God first over any other priority concerning my time or money and He will provide and protect me."*

My treasurer told me he felt God's anointing come over him, so he proceeded to walk straight toward this angry young man speaking words of peace while exalting Christ, all along asking the shooter to surrender his gun.

However the raging young man began firing his semi-automatic weapon hitting my treasurer in the arm. Moreover, at point blank range, firing twice more into his chest. Both bullets were direct hits; however, to everyone's amazement, the bullets hit him while leaving only two red marks.

My friend's testimony is: angels were sent by his Almighty God bringing protection that day just as he always professed. *Praise the LORD, you his angels, you mighty ones who do his bidding, who obey his word. Praise the LORD, all his heavenly hosts, you his servants who do his will.*[11]

I think you would agree with me that it took faith for my friend to leave his safety zone and get involved.

Again, faith isn't always pretty and glamorous. Of course our world only shows you the results of faith, never the dirty hard part that takes years to develop.

Upon the arrival of my first church to become the senior pastor, Jenny and I drove up to a very small white building out in the middle of nowhere called "Towes Chapel Church of God." The attendance was down to seven, and of course it could do nothing but go up in numbers. Right? Wrong. Upon my third week the head of the only family attending approached me. Quickly he yelled out with anger, "Next week we will have a choir!" I looked at him, and replied, "No we aren't going to do that." He began to threaten me by telling me what he would do if I didn't heed to his command. Faith rose up within me, and with the help of God I said, "Go ahead and quit. I'll cut the grass and wrap the pipes in the winter myself. I can handle it!"

Sadly, he and his family left. (It wasn't too sad though) From that time on, Jenny and I would stand on the front porch of that old church, and pray for people to come.

I began to pick up this sweet handicap man, and together we would roll down our windows as we traveled, and call the cows and the chickens to come and worship with us at Towes Chapel. **You've got to have fun in the midst of your battle.** Guess what? God sent people instead. However, I am convinced that the small church would not have grown off the charts without applying and standing through some hard faith zones. To God be the glory that little church that was established in 1936, grew to seventeen, and then thirty-five, seventy-five, one hundred, and before long over two hundred in attendance!

I challenged our people with excitement to tell someone about their church and they did. I even told them I would eat a can of English Peas(which I despise) and preach in my pajamas if they would tell their friends to come. In other words, I would do something radical if they would do the normal, and just invite people. What? Yes, inviting friends and family to church should be the norm.

We were able to relocate, buy new property, and build a new worship facility. Till this day, the church body thrives!

Remember this, real faith is usually (always) dirty, difficult and hard before any productivity is seen. Therefore roll your sleeves up, and get ready to rumble, so you can experience an adventure of a lifetime. *They were too good for this world, wandering over deserts and mountains, hiding in caves and holes in the ground.*[12]

Again, I want to stress, if someone says to you, "well it's easy," and they try to convince you their faith bought some type of instant fame, don't believe them. In fact, run. Somewhere down the line, someone paid a heavy price for their so called, "instant success."

Difficulty and failure can feel like a punch in the gut. And when it keeps happening it's tempting just to give up. But you can't; you must get up again. Failing doesn't make you a failure, quitting does. H.E. Jensen once said, *"The man who wins may have been counted out several times, but he didn't hear the referee."*[13] A failure-free life feels safe, but it fosters boredom, apathy and a low self-esteem.

Once I had a man come to my office, and he said to me, "I hate my job!" My rebuttal was, "why don't you leave and do something you would enjoy, you're more than qualified?" I'll never forget his response; "In eleven years my company will give me a gold watch, so I'm holding on." In my opinion no watch is worth misery.

All these people earned a good reputation because of their faith, yet none of them received all that God had promised. For God had something better in mind for us, so that they would not reach perfection without us.[14] If you are in Christ and you trust Him, my friend, you are walking in the full promises of God. So remember, it only gets grander as you arrive in front of the heavenly gates made of pearl.

Live faith, speak faith and do faith. You serve a God of abundance, so take the limits off of Him and unchain your thoughts. Come on go with me on this faith journey.

Questions
Can be answered in a group, or as an individual

What is faith?

Do you have a daily faith walk?

How can I grow in my faith walk?

What is sure in my life?

What am I in love with?

Would you follow God's plan whatever the cost?

What do I expect out of the next 12 months?

Five years?

How bout right now, what changes or adjustments can I make?

Chapter 2

The Value of Committal

Is anyone among you suffering? Let him pray.

Is anyone cheerful? Let him sing psalms.

Is anyone among you sick? Let him call for the elders of the church, and let them pray over him, anointing him with oil in the name of the Lord. And the prayer of faith will save the sick, and the Lord will raise him up.

And if he has committed sins, he will be forgiven. Confess your trespasses to one another, and pray for one another, that you may be healed.

The effective, fervent prayer of a righteous man avails much. Elijah was a man with a nature like ours, and he prayed earnestly that it would not rain; and it did not rain on the land for three years and six months. And he prayed again, and the heaven gave rain, and the earth produced its fruit.

James 5:13-18 NKJ

The New Testament has a specific word for every believer to pay attention to, and that word is, believe. If you desire to be healed, or if you need a miracle you have to believe.

I can't tell you how many times I have heard someone say, "I believe, or I'm claiming this or that," only to watch this same person forget all about God's promises, and negate them by their words and actions. It's time to believe, yes the time is now. Believe now, let go of your doubts and skepticism and just believe. If God can be believed, nothing is impossible. God is a miracle God; He always responds to faith.

"If God can be believed, nothing is impossible."

If you have been toying with the subject of healing, and experimenting with God, end it, and commit yourself in faith and love to Jesus Christ as your healer, forever. Then you have placed yourself on the ground of blessing. You have placed yourself where the Lord meets you; or rather you meet the Lord.[1]

My thought is committal, it means the burial of a corpse. However another definition is, the action of sending a person to an institution, or prison or a psychiatric hospital.[2] Sounds pretty rough- doesn't it?

Committal sounds final, at least until something or a someone has changed, and turned about face.

I'm afraid many people are no more than a lot of talk. Some are selfish, full of a lot of wind, and many laugh only to cover their pain. Whatever the next fad is, these people are onboard.

Hear this word, *"Unbelief expands just as faith grows, but the wind of God's spirit is all around the person of faith, and truly nothing is impossible."*

God is a God of committal. For example: His salvation is for a lifetime. His commission for His chosen is to go and make disciples of men. In Genesis, God said no more will I flood the whole earth. Moreover, in the New Testament, Jesus paid the price for sin once and for all. Of course this is just a few examples, through out God's word. The Lord shows Himself to be all about committal, so I declare to you, likewise, that you should be too.

" God is a God of committal."

Therefore as you read you see that to commit something is definite and sure. It should be forever, and it's not something you take back.

As you commit something to God, remember His covenant with you. He doesn't take back His love. He's committed to you forever, so why would you take back what you committed to Him? Why would you hold anything back from the Creator?

Right off the bat, as you review the verses in James 5, you see that James asked three questions, and then he answers them. *Is anyone among you suffering?* James gives you a definite answer, *pray.*

Prayer is not melodramatic whining and crying. It's not about emotions. Prayer that prevails is solid faith in God. It's a lifestyle of dialoging with the invisible hand of God. Believing God's word is final, breathed upon, plus it's heavenly.

In other words, the Bible isn't from this world. *All Scripture is given by inspiration of God, and is profitable for doctrine, for reproof, for correction, for instruction in righteousness, that the man of God may be* complete, thoroughly equipped for every good work.[3]

"The Bible isn't from this world."

Is anyone cheerful? Let him sing psalms. Singing the psalms brings reflection, and even purpose that goes into your cause. The greatest antidote in any given situation is to stay cheerful. Never respond to an important matter while sad or angry.

Don't live carelessly, unthinkingly. Make sure you understand what the Master wants. Don't drink too much wine. That cheapens your life. Drink the Spirit of God, huge draughts of him. Sing hymns instead of drinking songs! Sing songs from your heart to Christ. Sing praises over everything, any excuse for a song to God the Father in the name of our Master, Jesus Christ.[4]

Your praise can and will change the atmosphere. Also it will alter you, so in return your cheer touches the Master, not to mention how it rubs off on others.

Let's go farther with this thought; singing the psalms in a literal sense produces faith and courage. Right now, stop what you are doing and sing aloud in a prayerful mode Psalm 23, 1, 37, 40, 150 or 91. This is just a few of my favorites.

If you will begin to pray the psalm you will touch the heart of God, and those things you are committing unto Him will be settled.

The third question asked in scripture is, "Is anyone among you sick?" James gives us the solution to the cure. Before I go any farther I want to go back to that word committal again. *A.B. Simpson says concerning the committal of the health of our bodies to the Lord: "It ought to be very deliberate and final, and in the nature of things it cannot be repeated."*[5] In other words, when you give your cares or sickness unto the Lord don't dare take it back. Leave it in His hands. Then Rev. Simpson said something I can't leave out of this book. He said, *"If you commit yourself once and for all, and forever to Jesus as your healer, it is done forever.*[6]

Why not confess that Christ is your healer? Right now, consider it done, because Jesus Christ paid the price for your sins and sickness' once and forever.

Back in July 2000, I was called to the hospital one Sunday afternoon. Upon arrival I was told that the man I was to see was brain dead, and the hospital staff was just waiting for the family to give them permission to unplug all life support. As I entered the ICU ward his granddaughters who attended my church were around his bed.

One of the ladies asked me to pray; moreover, she proceeded to tell me their granddaddy had never given his life unto Jesus Christ, and all three granddaughters were concerned about his eternal home.

I began to pray with my eyes opened. His granddaughters agreed with me in a prayer of faith asking God to show this man mercy and give him one more chance to be born from above.

I asked the man if he could hear my prayer, to respond by moving his fingers. He moved one finger, and as I prayed again he began to wiggle his hand. God had responded, and showed compassion for him, but more than that, toward his granddaughters that understood the consequences of hell.

Finally, this old man came all the way back fully aware of his surroundings, and suddenly the Lord prompted me to tell his three granddaughters to lead their grandfather to salvation. They did, and they were elated that they had the opportunity to be a part of such an honor.

I am asking you right now, "What will you lose if you dare to believe?" I have seen firsthand miracles that I will share with you later.

Are any of you sick? You should call for the elders of the church to come and pray over you, anointing you with oil in the name of the Lord. Such a prayer offered in faith will heal the sick, and the Lord will make you well. And if you have committed any sins, you will be forgiven. Confess your sins to each other and pray for each other so that you may be healed. 7

I am going to say something that won't be popular, but here it goes. *"I cannot believe how some folks say salvation is enough, and they are on their way to heaven, but you can't find any faith words or actions coming from their lives. Their fruit seems to be spoiled and decayed. They are always down in their mouth and seem angry at the world.*

It also bothers me to hear some so-called full gospel followers who seem to be terribly doubled minded." One day these faithless followers seem so full, and then another day empty. Their words can't be trusted, and their prayers are vain. They're loud and seem to have a strong level of spirituality at church, but when they're alone, or find themselves in a fix, their true colors are seen and heard.

Hear this word, God the Father, Jesus Christ and the Holy Spirit have been given to each believer till Christ returns, and the trinity isn't confused. God is sure to anoint those that are faithful through their thoughts, and with their words and actions.

"The Godhead awaits the believer who dares to just believe."

What am I saying? "If you are sick get serious, change your associations, place scriptures on the walls, in your car or elsewhere. Begin to share in communion. Remember His benefits and the curse He bore for you. *Bless the LORD, O my soul; And all that is within me, bless His holy name! Bless the LORD, O my soul, And forget not all His benefits Who forgives all your iniquities, Who heals all your diseases,*[8]

So when you call upon an elder to anoint you with oil, and pray the prayer of faith keep your mind fixed on God's word. Decide right now that you are not going to be doubled minded meaning, a person with two minds or thought patterns about themselves and or God's word.

You, my friend, decide how much you really want from God. *"What if I don't get healed Pastor Howard?"* What if you do? Also, wouldn't you rather go to heaven living and speaking faith as your testimony? Don't hold up a white flag saying things like, *"Oh well, the devil's got me, I'm not worthy, I'm not good enough to be healed."* Stop it! If you are going to be a believer, then be a believer.

When you commit something to the Lord leave it there. Don't dare pick it back up again; don't dare quit or get mad with God. God gets blamed for everything, but the truth is, He's a good God. I want you to hear some scriptures that will prove God's compassion for His people and for you.

Now a leper came to Him, imploring Him, kneeling down to Him and saying to Him, "If

You are willing, You can make me clean."
Then Jesus, moved with compassion,
stretched out His hand and touched him, and
said to him, "I am willing; be cleansed."⁹

And when Jesus went out He saw a great
multitude; and He was moved with
compassion for them, and healed their sick.¹⁰
Jesus had compassion over one leper, just as
He did over the multitude. Jesus was never too
busy for the one, and that's pretty amazing.

Jesus' mission while on earth was to save and
heal mankind. He became our example on how
we should have compassion.

James 5 teaches you to have faith in God, so
before you ask others for prayer, you, in
return, should decide on a strong faith level for
yourself.

God's word teaches that every believer has a
measure of faith, but faith is suppressed when
so-called believers speak doubt and distrust in
God's promises because of their rotten
attitude, or their present issues with sin.

Sounds as though this word from James is
definite. ...*Confess your sins to each other and*
pray for each other so that you may be healed.
The earnest (heartfelt, continued) prayer of a

righteous man makes tremendous power available [dynamic in its working].[11]

As I'm praying for myself, I pray honest, faith filled prayers. I'm not into hearing myself or trying to be real loud. No, for me it's about being real and telling Jesus what I need. Of course I do this with emotions; however, I do not desire for my emotions to get in the way of faith. Faith and emotions are on different playing fields.

I say this with all sincerity, many allow their emotions to control every given situation, and God can't bless emotional flesh.

Once I was going through a time of depression. A man, who I had never met, came to my office discerning a problem; he asked if he could pray for me. He asked for my hand and said something like this, *"Lord right now, touch this pastor, and allow him to be free. Amen."* I was free, because of this man's obedience and faith. Once again, our faith, not our emotions, moves God.

No prayer is ever lost, or is any prayer ever breathed in vain. There is no such thing as prayer unanswered or unnoticed by God, and some things we see as refusals or denials are simply delays. Horatius Bonar[12]

"Faith and emotions are on different playing fields."

Elijah was as human as we are, and yet when he prayed earnestly that no rain would fall, none fell for three and a half years! Then, when he prayed again, the sky sent down rain and the earth began to yield its crops.[13]

James knew the tendency for most people is to place others on a pedestal, so he mentions that Elijah's passions were like our. He was a man; however not to belittle his accomplishments, he was a man of strong faith. What James is trying to get through to you is, *"If Elijah can pray and have results, you can too."*

I want you to commit some things over to the Lord right now. You should go ahead and have a committal service, and have a funeral. You don't have to wait for a pastor to do it at your own wake, you can take this faith matter and place it into His hands right now.

Pray this with me, *"Lord, I'm hungry for more of You, so I commit my body to Your service by faith. I will have faith, do faith, and speak faith from this day forward Amen."*

Questions

Can be answered in a group, or as an individual

What do you need to commit unto the Lord?

What do you daily confess?

What songs do you sing in your head during the day?

What moves your heart with compassion?

How often do you pray?

Chapter 3

Faith In The Battlefield

It happened in the spring of the year, at the time when kings go out to battle, that David sent Joab and his servants with him, and all Israel; and they destroyed the people of Ammon and besieged Rabbah. But David remained at Jerusalem.

2 Samuel 11:1 NKJ

Satan and his cohorts have strategies, and will not play fair; fair isn't even listed in their vocabulary. The devil is a liar and the prince of lies. How do you know when the devil is lying? When his lips are moving. He longs to play his demonic games inside your mind, and all he needs is an uncommitted will and off he goes.

He doesn't say things like, *"hey I'm the devil, and I want to control you, and maybe even kill you."* No, he say's things like, *"they don't like you, or why attend church, why care, you will only get hurt."*

".....he lies only when his lips are moving."

David didn't get into trouble until he left the battlefield. When he stopped fighting, he suffered his greatest defeat. The sad part of David's escapade was, there was given *"great occasion to the enemies of the Lord to blaspheme."* If you have failure in your life the devil gets to brag throughout the land. And oh you better believe he does.

However, faith in God throughout any battle you face will defeat your foes. Our human nature calls for perfection maybe because it was God's first plan for man-kind to live and dwell in Eden. However, after the fall, mankind still strived for perfection, but of course it wasn't possible.

Through Christ we are to fight the good fight of faith. Presently your protection depends on you staying in the right place. Remaining faithful at your post, and don't give the enemy an inch because he'll take a mile. Keep your sword drawn and your shield of faith high.

"Keep your sword drawn and your shield of faith high."

In Ephesians six, Paul writes about our armor. He even relates this armor to the Roman days as soldiers went out for battle to protect Rome.

It's important to notice as you study Ephesians six, there's no armor for the soldiers backside. Why? Because he couldn't turn and run, and if he thought fighting was tough, wait till he sees what happens if he stops.

Let's look farther at Ephesians and relate it to us, *Finally, my brethren, be strong in the Lord* and in the power of His might. Put on the whole armor of God, that you may be able to stand against the wiles of the devil. For we do not wrestle against flesh and blood, but against principalities, against powers, against the rulers of the darkness of this age, against spiritual hosts of wickedness in the heavenly places.

Therefore take up the whole armor of God, that you may be able to withstand in the evil day, and having done all, to stand. Stand therefore, having girded your waist with truth, having put on the breastplate of righteousness, and having shod your feet with the preparation of the gospel of peace; above all, taking the shield of faith with which you will be able to quench all the fiery darts of the wicked one. And take the helmet of salvation, and the sword of the Spirit, which is the word of God; praying always with all prayer and supplication in the Spirit, being watchful to this end with all perseverance and supplication for all the saints— and for me, that utterance may be given to me, that I may open my mouth boldly to make known the mystery of the gospel, for which I am an *ambassador in chains; that in it I may speak boldly, as I ought to speak.[1]*

Right from the start, you need to know that you are serving a Mighty God. His power isn't inferior, or second rate. I have seen the hand of God do the impossible; I have seen Him save the worse of sinners.

Back in 1989, I was in line at a grocery store to pay for some milk for our young son while Jenny stayed in the car. We had been in a revival service, so naturally I was walking in a strong level of faith. As I approached the cashier without even realizing it, I was humming a praise tune.

The cashier said to me, *"you sure are happy tonight."* Without even thinking, I answered back, *"well, I have the joy of the Lord within me!"* She looked at me and tearfully said, *"I want that."* Excitedly, I looked around because I knew God had opened this effectual door to lead her into salvation. Finally I spotted the night manager, and asked him if I could walk his cashier outside and have prayer with her. He consented, so she followed me.

As I began to pray for her, seemingly out of nowhere, ten or more people from the same revival had gathered around. We talked with her, and continued to have more prayer.

She came to faith in Jesus Christ and was moved upon by His powerful Spirit in a mighty way. Come to find out, she had been living in her car, because of years of alcohol addiction, but that night Jesus Christ saved her and set her free. Furthermore, she became strong in the Lord from that day on.

Paul tells us to put on the whole armor of God. Nowhere in scripture will you find that you are to take if off. God's armor is forever and the longer you wear it the more you realize it's importance.

I'm a chaplain for our county sheriff department. As I ride with the officers they tell me the same thing. *"These bullet proof vests are very hot and uncomfortable, but we have to wear them because it can save our life."* However, God's armor brings spiritual protection which the believer can't afford to live without.

Notice also as you wear this armor you will understand the wiles, tactics or schemes of the devil. It's very important to discern right from wrong spiritually. Sometimes things look right, but they are dead wrong. When believers begin to take their spiritual armor for granted, they in turn forget the liar's ways and tragedy can occur.

"Human ability, dynamic personalities, titles, and designer clothes don't impress God. He respects people who, when they get knocked down, bounce back with their faith intact, more determined than ever to live for Him."

We should understand that people are people, and they will make mistakes. However, at the same time remember that you aren't warring against flesh and blood; you are in direct conflict with principalities and powers on high. We war against spirits even in high places; however, remember Jesus Christ is the head over all principalities, and you are complete in Christ. (Col.2, 10) If you will stay completely submitted to Jesus the enemy can't divert God's plan for your life. You might ask, *"how do I know if I am totally submitted?"* My answer back to you is, *"if you have faith and believe; you are on your way."*

"The enemy can't divert God's plan for your life."

Therefore, put on every piece of God's armor so you will be able to resist the enemy in the time of evil. Then after the battle you will still be standing firm. Stand your ground, putting on the belt of truth and the body armor of God's righteousness.² Every piece; this doesn't mean you go around worrying, *"do I have every piece of God's armor on?"* No, you wear God's armor by faith. *But without faith it is impossible to please him: for he that cometh to God must believe that he is, and that he is a rewarder of them that diligently seek him.³*

Just as a believer stands in faith alone, the Romans soldier wore shoes built for battle. These shoes were difficult to take off and put on, and had tremendous ankle support; in addition, the bottom of these shoes had half-inch spikes. These spikes would keep the solider on solid ground regardless. For instance, if a soldier were forced to go backwards because of enemy pressure it would nearly be impossible. They could only go forward, or fall forward in faith.

Also this brought every Roman solider instant peace having sure footing over their enemies at all times.

"The belt of truth goes around every believer; it represents a circle of truth that cannot be broken. As God's word is trusted, it can be leaned upon; likewise, this belt of truth keeps you secure. As you live with the belt of truth you don't have to worry because you can feel God's help."

God is our refuge and strength, A very present help in trouble.[4]

The Roman belt was used to hang other weapons on as well as to keep the soldier's armor in tact or from falling off.

Then Paul writes about our loins girded about with truth. Even though this small piece of equipment seemed little it was stationed in the middle section below the warrior's navel, and of course this was a very delicate area. Of course, while in your mother's womb, this was the very cord that supplied you with nourishment. Also, for the soldier, all his equipment was attached here. Your loin area is also part of your center of gravity.

The top part of all the soldiers' equipment, and the lower part of his equipment came together at the loins. *"Isn't that what God's truth does for every believer?"* His word lights our way, and keeps us on the straight and narrow path.

"Without the truth being the center of all the believer does, nothing works right."

As you wear the breastplate of righteousness you understand that your life isn't your own. You quickly come to the realization that its Christ are nothing. If it were not for the righteousness of God, your sins would be retained and there wouldn't be any hope.

For He made Him who knew no sin to be sin for us, that we might become the righteousness of God in Him.[5] I will always be in awe of this one scripture. It's humanly impossible to grasp the love Jesus has for mankind. Without the breastplate of righteousness the believer won't understand their instructions, nor will they carry out the plans God has for them with confidence. It's important that every believer understands and even speaks out, "I am the righteousness of God."

Once again the shoes of peace are the shoes that keeps each believer secure. As you wear the shoes of peace, no matter what satan throws at you, peace will come upon you; the peace that passes all understanding.

Remember, no soldier would go out to war without his shoes. Relating this to every believer, wearing the shoes of peace means you can walk forward, and yes you will come against some difficult objects and foes, but these shoes will keep you from falling.

The shield of faith holds back every firing assault of the devil. The Roman shield wasn't small; it nearly covered every part of the soldier's vital organs. This shield was always carried in battle. No soldier stood a chance without the shield. It brought instant protection from the firing darts of the enemy. This shield was very thick and could not be penetrated unless the soldier dropped it.

The enemy would literally shoot arrows that had been soaked with a solvent. This would make the tip of the arrow burn through the air causing mass destruction. However as long as the soldier kept their shield of faith in position these fiery arrows couldn't complete their mission. That's exactly what faith will do for you. Faith is to be spoken and acted upon at all times.

In Roman days every soldier wore a helmet in battle. These helmets were designed to protect the head, and even around the face area. Some had sharp points that could do damage and even kill the enemy.

Not only was the helmet meant to protect, it also displayed beautiful feathers of all different colors. The soldier with the highest rank, as well as the warrior with many kills, had the most adorned helmets. Peacock feathers waving around in the air, was a sign to the by standers and fellow soldiers, of their value.

Isn't it that way with the Lord's salvation? You will flow with confidence as you grow in the depths of Jesus' righteousness.

Many believers aren't aware of this, but the salvation you have obtained and wear, should be beautiful to the world. It should always wave and display salvation. One more time, the salvation you carry is grand and it most certainly wasn't cheap. Christ paid for it with His own precious blood!

As you wear your salvation proudly, you should carry the sword of the spirit as a sword of peace. Most importantly it is a weapon of defense. Remember it's a two edged sword. You have the authority and ability to keep the enemy at bay. Again remember according to Hebrews, the sword is sharp on both sides. You don't have to turn this heavy sword to the left or right- you just swing and speak God's precious word, it will get the job done. Just speak and believe.

It will cut, convict, deliverer, bring fruit or miracles on any given occasion.

"Speak faith, it has the ability to cut right through the strategies of the devil."

God's word is very clear on what every believer should do next, they pray. And when they pray their prayers are powerful. Regardless of what is happening, pray boldly and with confidence. Jesus Christ is seated on the right hand of Father God making intercession for everyone that believes. Dump everything over on the Lord He can handle it, moreover He desires no less from you.

Remember in the last part of Ephesians six, Paul calls himself an ambassador who carries the glorious gospel of Christ. Can I remind you that you too are an ambassador for Christ Jesus?

As you wear God's full armor, you can rest assured, you will do and say the right thing. God's best has been given to you, so wear it confidently.

I have a friend who travels a lot. One thing I know about him is that he understands who he is in Christ. As my friend sat in yet another plane, someone inevitably asks him what he does for a living? He tells them, *"I'm a foreign ambassador."* Of course this attracts a lot of attention, and it opens the door for him to tell the person about his chief in command.

So what are you waiting for? Put on God's full armor!

We are pressed on every side by troubles, but we are not crushed. We are perplexed, but not driven to despair. We are hunted down, but never abandoned by God. We get knocked down, but we are not destroyed.[6]

You've failed many times although you may not remember. This article ran in The Wall Street Journal: "You fell the first time you tried to walk. You almost drowned the first time you tried to swim. Did you hit the ball the first time you swung the bat? Heavy hitters, the ones who hit the most home runs, also strike out a lot. R.H. Macy failed seven times before his store in New York caught on. English novelist John Creasey got 753 rejection slips before publishing 564 books."[7]

Once again, *"Don't make the same mistake David did, go out to battle."* Don't just show up and be counted. Decide today that you are going to make a difference. That you are going to walk and talk on the highest level you possibly can and that level is faith.

Dr. Theodore Rubin says, 'The problem is not that there are problems, it's expecting otherwise; it's thinking that having problems is the problem!' There are no perfect situations in life. You need courage to face whatever comes, to realize that what you can't solve, you can out-last and out-love![8]

So whether you're getting up, or lying down, right now put your armor on.

Paul writes ...*that in it I may speak boldly, as I ought to speak. Christ sometimes delays His help so He may test our faith and energize our prayers. Our boat may be tossed by the waves while He continues to sleep, but He will awake before it sinks. He sleeps but He never oversleeps, for He is never too late. Alexander Maclaren* [9]

Questions

Can be answered in a group, or as an individual

Do you think of yourself as a warrior?

By faith, do you make daily professions?

Do you suffer with condemnation?

Do you have daily peace?

What's your spiritual strength?

How bout your weakness'

Chapter 4

I Shall Not Want - Faith Is Rest

The LORD is my shepherd; I shall not want. He makes me to lie down in green pastures;

He leads me beside the still waters. He restores my soul; He leads me in the paths of righteousness For His name's sake. Yea, though I walk through the valley of the shadow of death, I will fear no evil; For You are with me; Your rod and Your staff, they comfort me.

You prepare a table before me in the presence of my enemies; You anoint my head with oil; My cup runs over.

Surely goodness and mercy shall follow me All the days of my life; And I will dwell in the house of the LORD Forever.

Psalm 23:1-6NKJ

*P*salm twenty-three is one of the most beloved psalms, and as far as that goes, it's one of the most beloved chapters in the Bible.

However, given the time and day David penned this psalm we should look further into it, and glean from these statements of faith and surety.

The first thing you will notice is that there is a direct person this psalm is writing to. Those who have chosen to trust and place their confidence in the Lord. There are many personal pronouns in Psalm 23, and that is just one reason this psalm is so beloved. Whoever reads this passage can place their name in these six verses.

David proclaims right off, the Lord is my shepherd. Christ is a shepherd who will leave ninety-nine and save the one sheep that has gone astray. He is a shepherd who will rescue one of His own in danger. It doesn't matter if you are in the company of thousands, God will personally take care of you. Speak and claim that right now. *"The Lord is my shepherd."* The word shepherd was commonly used in kingly applications, and is frequently ascribed to Jesus in the New Testament.

"Christ is a shepherd who will leave ninety-nine and save the one sheep that has gone astray."

David made this proclamation, **"I shall not want,"** not because he was prosperous and full in every way, but because he was satisfied and that his God was so near. *God, my shepherd! I don't need a thing. You have bedded me down in lush meadows,[1]* Real success begins and ends in Christ. Becoming satisfied, running over, filled to the brim while sloshing the spirit on others- now that's living.

Back in June of 2002 before Sunday morning church I was hungry, so I stopped at this great breakfast place to order a sausage biscuit with coffee. I was third in line, so after I ordered, I then reached for my billfold to no avail. *"Oh no, I had forgotten my billfold."*

Before I ordered, I had been anticipating the morning message mixed with prayer over our service. I thought to myself, *"Well I guess I better pull out of the line, and move onward towards church."*

Suddenly, I honestly felt the spirit of the Lord

tell me to open my door, I did and to my surprise there were coins all around my car door. I can remember looking around to see if anyone was watching, I felt as though the heavens opened just for me! God as my wittiness, I needed $3.27, and on the ground laid $3.27 exactly. It might not have been much money, but God knew actually what I needed. You talk about getting my food and being grateful- I will never forget that morning, or the sermon I preached after that simple but great event.

"As a believer do you really have any wants?"

Psalm twenty-three progressively unveils David's personal relationship with the Lord in three stages. First David's exclamation: The Lord is my shepherd. Secondly, David's expectations: I shall not want, and I shall fear no evil. Finally, David's exultation: My cup runs over.

Before we go any farther, I ask you the question, *"Is God your shepherd?"* If not, what are you waiting on? David proclaims, *"I shall not want."*

In the past, the shepherd has spoken to me to give away something valuable on several occasions, and come to find out it would be just what that ministry or person needed.

If you will allow God the chance to speak to you He will do the same for you and through you.

Once again as senior pastor of Crane Eater Community Church I heard the inner voice speak to me back in 2005 when I took the pastorate of this great church that was established in 1914. He said, *"You will be sent here to build, and grow the body and a new worship facility."*

He also gave me three powerful words to inscribe within the hearts of His people. *"We are to be a people of Love, Prayer and Grace."*

I don't think I would hear His voice with clarity if I weren't open to hear His voice when He tells me to sacrifice something of importance.

Remember a true servant of God hears and heeds to God's voice through the good and bad times. Sometimes hearing His voice costs, but His benefits far out weigh everything. Maybe I should ask you right now, *"are you willing to hear His voice and even sacrifice?"*

I shall not want. Sounds spiritual doesn't it? *And my God shall supply all your need according to His riches in glory by Christ Jesus.*[2] Paul expressly says, He will supply our needs, however when you are in Christ your wants and your needs are usually closely related. In other words, you don't live in a dreamland.

Strong faith is vital and this kind of faith is essential. The person who has the Lord as their shepherd will have their priorities in check.

David's writes, my shepherd- emphasizing His grace and guidance makes me lie down in green pastures. Simply put, I don't know if you have ever gotten the chance to lie down in luscious tall green grass right dab in the middle of a field, but there's nothing like it. Feeling the cool green grass on your backside while staring at the clouds in the sky. You will never be more content than you are as you lay there. It's not that the Lord makes you lie down, but once you get in His presence you get to lie down.

Also His pastures represent His rest and peace on the inside. Listen my friend; there is peace, comfort and joy in Christ. In John chapter ten, Christ is called the Good Shepherd. He gives everyone who chooses the ability to lie down in green pastures with everything he or she needs, and what mankind really needs and truly desires is rest with contentment. Christ is the door or gate, so while you go through His gate He protects and satisfies. He allows you to enter one pasture and then another, He fulfills your every need.

Have you ever been driving and seen landscape, maybe some lush pasture land with valley's and hill's it seemed to suck you right in, and you dreamed of living there?

My wife Jenny was given this poem from the Lord right before a Good Friday service in 2010 *"Weight of sin, more than ever. Guilt within, more than ever, punishment, more than ever, help us Lord, help us Lord. Angry crowd, more than ever, confused world, more than ever. Doubt and fear, more than ever, we need you Lord, we need you Lord. A cross to bear, more than ever, crown of thorns, more*

than ever, nail pierced hands, more than ever.
We love you Lord, we love you Lord. Grace
and mercy, more than ever, souls saved, more
than ever, His blood delivers, more than
ever. Thank you Lord, Thank you Lord!"

As the shepherd leads, the believer is taught
to express his satisfaction in the care of the
great Pastor of the universe, the Redeemer and
Preserver of mankind. With joy he reflects that
he has a shepherd, and that his shepherd is
Jehovah. *A flock of sheep, gentle and*
harmless, feeding in verdant pastures, under
the care of a skillful, watchful, and tender
shepherd, forms an emblem of believers
brought back to the Shepherd of their souls.
The greatest abundance is but a dry pasture
to a wicked man, who relishes in it only what,
pleases the senses; but to a godly man, who by
faith tastes the goodness of God in all his
enjoyments, though he has but little of the
world, it is a green pasture. The Lord gives
quiet and contentment in the mind, whatever
the lot is.[3]

"With joy David reflects that he has a shepherd, and that shepherd is

Jehovah."

*...You find me quiet pools to drink from.
True to your word, you let me catch my
breath and send me in the right direction.*
⁴Peaceful streams, is there any stream that
isn't peaceful?

A few months ago, Jenny and I traveled
almost one hundred miles only to watch a
beautiful waterfall, and the beauty was truly
worth the drive. We decided to follow the falls
upstream, and to our amazement this powerful
sounding fall came from a relatively small
stream. In fact if a person didn't realize it, they
surly wouldn't believe that stream could
generate such a tremendous waterfall.
However, it's not the strength of the stream,
it's the height of the drop. Many times in life
you don't gain momentum until you go down,
or go through some huge hurdles.

*"Wishing to encourage her young son's
progress on the piano, a mother took him to a
Paderewski concert. After they were seated,
the mother spotted a friend in the audience
and walked down the aisle to greet her.*

Meanwhile, the little boy seized the opportunity to explore the wonders of the concert hall and eventually explored his way through the door marked 'no admittance.'

"When the house lights dimmed and the concert was about to begin, the mother made her way back to her seat and discovered that her son was missing. Suddenly, the curtains parted and spotlights focused on the impressive Steinway piano on the stage. In horror, the mother saw her little boy sitting at the keyboard innocently picking out 'Twinkle, Twinkle Little Star.'

"At that moment, the great piano master made his entrance and moved quickly to the piano and whispered into the child's ear, 'Don't quit. Keep playing!' Then, leaning over, Paderewski reached down with his left hand and began filling in the bass part. Soon, the right arm reached around the other side of the boy and added a running obligato.

Together, the old master and the young novice transformed a frightening situation into a wonderfully creative experience. The audience was mesmerized."5

Quiet pools to drink from, this reminds me of the words of Jesus as He came to Jerusalem and found a fountain of water that was used in those days for purification; however, this day it's used as a reference referring to after Jesus' own death, burial and resurrection. How the Holy Spirit would change everything.

I can picture Him holding up a cup of water dipped from the fountain. He says, *now on the final and most important day of the Feast, Jesus stood, and He cried in a loud voice, If any man is thirsty, let him come to Me and drink! He who believes in Me [who cleaves to and trusts in and relies on Me] as the Scripture has said, From his innermost being shall flow [continuously] springs and rivers of living water.*[6]

David refers to this by writing, when I'm weary and can't go any farther, my Lord brings me refreshment as I lay down, rest and trust in Him. I can hear him say, *"It's as though the Lord Himself brings the water just for me, and only for me as I rest. Before I realize it, this spring of refreshment bubbles up, and out of me onto everything I do, and I can continue my journey in the right direction through out my life."*

Little did David know that one day God's anointing would come upon him in such form that he would become a giant killer. Always remember though before David killed Goliath, he had proven to be a killer of large game.

"It's as though the Lord Himself brings the water just for me, and only for me as I rest."

He refreshes and restores my life (my self); He leads me in the paths of righteousness [uprightness and right standing with Him-- not for my earning it, but] for His name's sake.[7] Everything that is accomplished through your life comes because of Christ. As you trust Him you will find a peace you didn't earn, nor deserve. Whenever you fall or feel like a complete mess, just remember Jesus' blood being shed once, paid in full for your sins. If you can learn to confess and lean on Jesus' righteousness, oh what a difference it will make. I want you to make a new faith declaration right now, although you might not need it presently. *"Jesus made me righteous, and He did it once and forever."* Make this your daily confession. You might think and even say, *"I'm not righteous."* My friend, remember it's all about Jesus.

"I am the righteousness of God."

Yes, though I walk through the [deep, sunless] valley of the shadow of death, I will fear or dread no evil, for You are with me; Your rod [to protect] and Your staff [to guide], they comfort me.[8] I found this in an email that was sent to me from David Barnes, and deemed it worthy for this section of the book. "What Cancer Can't Do." *Though the physical body may be destroyed, the spirit remains triumphant. Cancer is such a dreaded thing, and it seems so powerful, but cancer is limited. It cannot cripple Love, It cannot shatter hope, It cannot corrode faith, It cannot destroy friendship, It cannot kill confidence, It cannot shut out memories, It cannot silence courage, It cannot invade your soul, It cannot reduce eternal life, It cannot quench God's Spirit, and It cannot lessen the power of the resurrection.*[9]

"Right now you can receive the bubbling pools of God's endless love, and live in the shadows of His protective custody."

Fear is always contrary to love, and God's love can, and will overwhelm any and all fear— past, present and future. Perfect love will cast fear into the pit of hell.

God's rod chastens, corrects and brings you back into submission always for your betterment. God's love is without any restraints; He's after your love, and He will go the entire journey with you. A good shepherd always protects his sheep, and carries his rod with him.

Another good prayer for you to pray daily is, *You who sit down in the High God's presence, spend the night in Shaddai's shadow,*[10]

Say this: "God, you're my refuge. I trust in you and I'm safe!" That's right—he rescues you from hidden traps, shields you from deadly hazards. His huge outstretched arms protect you—under them you're perfectly safe; his arms fend off all harm. Fear nothing —not wild wolves in the night, not flying arrows in the day, Not disease that prowls through the darkness, not disaster that erupts at high noon. Even though others succumb all around, drop like flies right and left, no harm will even graze you. You'll stand untouched, watch it all from a distance, watch the wicked turn into corpses. Yes, because God's your refuge, the High God your very own home, Evil can't get close to you, harm can't get through the door. He ordered his angels to guard you wherever you go. If you stumble, they'll catch you; their job is to keep you from falling. You'll walk unharmed among lions and snakes, and kick young lions and serpents from the path.[11]

God is always your able protector and abundant provider. Your staff [to guide], they comfort me.[12] God's staff today is the Holy Spirit. His spirit brings comfort, and can bring help to anyone who will call upon His name. God's spirit brings refreshment and a wholeness that offers new living authority.

Back in 1987, I had been riding horses all day. I was working as a trainer in Cartersville Georgia. As I rode, I would pray and seek God.

One Wednesday night my pastor taught a great word, and after the word he gave, he called everyone around the altar. As I began to pray and praise as others did the same, the Holy Spirit came upon me, and seemingly took me up out of my body. I could feel my body; however, I was keenly aware of my spirit up above me. It seemed as though I was about 30 feet in the air, and the best I can explain it is, *"I didn't want to come back."* I can even remember saying, *"Lord I don't want to go back, Lord, I don't want to go back."* I had a strong desire to go further. I could hear my pastor say, *"don't mind or bother Howard he's just getting a blessing."* And boy I sure did! Finally my spirit man entered back into my body. I can tell you this, I will never forget that Wednesday. The Holy Spirit is with us to bring elevation, so right now you can call for His help.

You serve me a six-course dinner right in front of my enemies. You revive my drooping head; my cup brims with blessing.[13] When you can eat in the midst of true enemies you know you are living in the grace of All Mighty God. Sure you will feel the heat, but as you drink your tea around the very people who talk about you, and the ones who backbite, that's God's mercy. As you stay in God's presence, He will remove all depression and even bring your confidence back.

When you belong to Christ you are immensely blessed. Your confession for yourself, as well as your family should begin to be filled with blessings, because God has deemed you worthy. Don't settle for less than the blessings of the Lord.

Remember David being chased by Saul? He never received Saul's spirit of hatred or jealousy- David refused it. David just kept eating His meals in the presence of His redeemer, and of course David eats, lives and even plays his stringed instrument in the midst of king Saul. That's the anointing.

Surely or only goodness, mercy, and unfailing love shall follow me all the days of my life, and through the length of my days the house of the Lord [and His presence] shall be my dwelling place. And I will dwell.[14] There is some question concerning the form in the Hebrew text. It should be rendered, *"I shall dwell?" Whichever way it is taken, by the grace of his Lord, David is expecting ongoing opportunities of intimate fellowship.*[15]

Brother Wayne Fauber a faithful man of God, was sharing with me the difference between grace and mercy, *"Grace is getting what you do not deserve. Mercy is not getting what you do deserve."*

Questions

Can be answered in a group, or as an individual

Is the Lord your shepherd? Really?

Do you have wants? What are they?

Do you have enemies?

Are you anointed?

Do you know you are the righteousness of God?

Do you sleep well at night?

Chapter 5

Grace Killers - Gaining Knowledge of The Father

"And he arose and came to his father. But when he was still a great way off, his father saw him and had compassion, and ran and fell on his neck and kissed him.

"Now his older son was in the field. And as he came and drew near to the house, he heard music and dancing. So he called one of the servants and asked what these things meant.

And he said to him, 'Your brother has come, and because he has received him safe and sound, your father has killed the fatted calf.'

"But he was angry and would not go in. Therefore his father came out and pleaded with him. So he answered and

said to his father, 'Lo, these many years I have been serving you; I never transgressed your commandment at any time; and yet you never gave me a young goat, that I might make merry with my friends.

But as soon as this son of yours came, who has devoured your livelihood with harlots, you killed the fatted calf for him.' "And he said to him, 'Son, you are always with me, and all that I have is yours. It was right that we should make merry and be glad, for your brother was dead and is alive again, and was lost and is found.'"

Luke 15: 20, 25-32 NLT

Putting a twenty first century twist to this story, a person could possibly think, *"these two boys had severe issues."* The younger brother could have been labeled as Bi-Polar while the older boy lived with severe anger issues. Today, both would be under a doctor's supervision, hopefully. However, Christ can change anyone who will choose to live submitted to Him.

Have you ever thought about those to whom Jesus spoke harshly, and even condemned? Was it the sinner? No, it was always the ones who knew better, but refused to give grace to others and themselves. They chose to live by the measure system, where no one could ever come close to them, or to their expectations.

Many times, those raised in the church or perhaps, those who slept under pews as children, could have a tendency to be cold and graceless. After all, they've known about it all their life and their relationship with Christ, as well as others, has been taken for granted.

"Those who slept under the pews could have a tendency to be cold and graceless."

Maybe they became sour because of life in general, and many times God gets blamed for anything and everything. Why not, He's convenient. Some have been burned by the so called, "church world." They label anyone attending church as their enemy or worse yet, hypocritical or crazy. Now the terminology is *"The far left."*

The story of the prodigal son represents a type of Christ, being the Father, who is waiting to save those who are lost. He is willing to restore, repair and heal anyone, no matter where they are in the scheme of life.

In contrast, is the judgmental person. A strong word that comes to mind and is hardly ever talked about, is presumption. It occurs when someone assumes to know everything about something or someone. Both are dangerous assumptions, because the person possessing this attitude can't be helped or taught.

Becoming familiar with people, places and things can stop the hand of a Mighty God. It also halts a servant of God in their tracks. It can keep the pastor from giving his congregation the proper word from God. Also, presumption can settle in within the congregation till they can't hear their own shepherd anymore: their ears and hearts have become spiritually plugged up. How sad.

Remember, Jesus didn't spend much time with these characters. Not because He didn't care, but because they usually thought they knew it all. They say things like, *"Why, I've known him for twenty years, way before he went to that medical school; he can't help me."* Or maybe, *"Well, she once was a wild one, I heard she a had a child out of wedlock, I surly don't believe she has changed."* Sadly, Graceless is their name.

You might be surprised to find several people you know with this attitude. Some, being in error, could have been raised believing certain facts about the Bible. They don't understand that God's word is living and powerful, so they limit themselves, and God, because of presumption.

I am not open-minded about farfetched ideas that aren't backed by God's word, or something that isn't practical or useful. I'd rather not hear about it; however, if it's found in the Word of God, I hunger for it. If it's information that can help me, or teach me something new, I'm in line; count me in.

Some of the larger retail stores now offer classes on, "how to repair something, or how to build what you want..." I think this way of thinking is very productive and fruitful and could serve the church world well.

Notice, verse *20 "And he arose and came to his father. But when he was still a great way off, his father saw him and had compassion, and ran and fell on his neck and kissed him.*

Finally, this young man's eyes opened to the fact that home wasn't so boring. Before he left, he was filled with presumption, but now the lad has learned a valuable lesson; life is hard and bills aren't fun to pay. "What I once assumed to be old, dull and common is everything I desire; patterns and devotions are good, and they do enhance and bring good discipline."

Remember this word, *"Your children need to see, so they can mimic, good patterns from your marriage and life in general."* It's wonderful when flashing lights, and bells resound within someone. It's also fantastic when something new is learned in an old-timer, or maybe just an old thinker who has decided long ago- *"I shall not change."* This speaks volumes to all that really thought there wasn't any hope for that particular person.

Also, it very well could be one of the greatest miracles of all. Wouldn't it be wonderful if the saying, *"You can't teach an old dog new tricks,"* was just a myth?

This young man came to understand that pig food couldn't sustain him and playing with the dogs infested him with fleas that bite and even suck blood. Sin drains the very life of God right out of you.

"Your children need to see, so they can mimic, good patterns from your marriage and life in general."

The boy made an effort; he walked and maybe even ran some. He arose and came to his father. I think I should point out, that this father never saw his son as a prodigal, he knew him by his God given name, "_____." His love was greater than any mistake he could ever make.

There's a story about a guy who fell into a pit and couldn't get out: *A subjective person came along and said, "I feel for you down there" An objective person came along and said, "Well, it's logical somebody would fall down there." A Pharisee said, "Only bad people fall into pits." A judgmental Christian said, "You deserve your pit." A realist said, "Now that's a pit." A geologist told him to appreciate the rock strata in the pit. A tax agent asked him if he was paying taxes on the pit. A self-pitying person said, "You haven't seen anything until you've seen my pit." An optimist said, "Things could be worse." A pessimist said, "Things will get worse." Jesus, seeing the guy in the pit, reached down, took him by the hand and lifted him out of the pit.[1]*

When this father caught a glimpse of his boy he wasn't thinking about punishment or any sort of discipline. No, he just wanted to get his hands on him, and express his true feelings of love mixed with action.

There isn't anything under the sun that replaces a real display of love.

I can give my children lecture after lecture, but I've learned that real genuine love can destroy every barrier faster than anything.

Your speech and actions have great potential to melt the coldest heart.

Sons and daughters alike hunger for those closest to them to become vulnerable, to be real, open and honest. Never be ashamed of tears that you might shed it could be the very emotion that touches your child's heart.

"I've learned that real genuine love can destroy every barrier faster than anything else."

This father allowed his true emotions to control him, he caught just one peek of his son and he took off running, he grabbed his son, picked him up, and the two began to spin around and around. As tears of joy flowed down the boy's neck, the old man shouted, *"My son's alive!"* The father and son fell to the ground, sobbing, with a new truce of love deep within.

This boy will never gamble or waste life again. He will be forever changed by his life experience.

Ask any head coach, or scout, and they will tell you that passion as a team player, will go further than a name or status. In addition, when a company finds a person with a degree and a compassionate attitude, they are most likely to hire that particular someone.

Here's the definition of compassion. *Compassion is a profound human emotion prompted by the pain of others, and more vigorous than empathy. The feeling commonly gives rise to an active desire to alleviate another's suffering.*[2]

Verse 25 "Now his older son was in the field. And as he came and drew near to the house, he heard music and dancing. This older son never left the fathers house; however, his mind and heart had become bitter, tired and cold. He deserved all the royal treatment he thought. After all, while his brother played, he worked and tended his father's animals.

As the days rolled by, the older brother played one film over and over in his mind. *"If I ever see this playboy brother of mine again, I am going to drop kick him. He's going to pay dearly for playing while I wait on this blankety blank father of mine!"* His soul raged within, it's obvious isn't it? His body was at home, but his heart had withdrawn some time ago. *Keep your heart with all diligence, for out of it spring the issues of life.*[3]

I believe this is a huge problem in many churches. There are several individuals with hardened hearts. While pastor preaches faith, hope and love, there are individuals who role-play one frame in their mind over and over again.

Some of these people are even teaching others while harboring a bitter spirit. These individuals can't enjoy anything they do, because their hearts and minds have checked out long ago. So, they go around once more, living with regret, heartache and pain. They were once done wrong, and so everyone has to pay for their excessive baggage.

With all honesty, I've felt like this older brother before, and it's sickening. *"Why the fun, cut the music off, don't you see this sling blade, mop and hammer in my hand, you can't have fun because I'm not."*
Many in the body have stopped dreaming. *"All men dream: but not equally. Those who*

dream by night in the dusty recesses of their minds wake in the day to find that it was vanity: but the dreamers of the day are dangerous men, for they may act their dreams with open eyes, to make it possible."
~T.E. Lawrence[4]

I think it's worse when the bitter person never vents; he or she just stews within. To make things worse, the older brother asked one of the hired hands what the commotion was all about? So he hears of his brother's return home from one of his father's hired hands and that adds insult to injury. In the back of his mind this is just another low blow.

He's filled with so much emotion he can't contain himself. So he belts out his real feelings, and anyone within earshot gets to hear everything. He vents, *"A fatted calf! Why, the old man hasn't ever done anything like that for me. I haven't wasted his money, I haven't slept and messed around with God knows what!"*

"His frame never left the farm, but his soul had long been checked out."

He hated everything that the farm, animals, and fields represented.

Sometimes mankind's emotions hit a ceiling, and everything that once brought satisfaction now represents misery and despair. If the facts were known, the older son really wished he were in the prodigal's position, and living it up; one party after another. He daydreams, but because he didn't respond and have the guts to leave, he turns his anger toward the one he envies. At least he can get the satisfaction of being righteous- self-righteous that is. *"The good church going boy with hate, and resentment in his heart."* Don't answer this question out loud, but do you know someone like this boy?

I believe we live in the generation that is spoiled and replaces needs with their wants. A people that hears just another sermon, or even sees just another miracle-God help us!

Grace is the only answer, receiving something you can't earn. Grace is- God's ability to do in you what you can't do for yourself. Sound good? That's grace.

John Newton's final months on this earth were difficult. However, upon losing most of his senses he would say, *"My memory is nearly gone; however, I remember two things: that I am a great sinner, and that Christ is a great Savior.*5

Remember, you can't give what you don't have. Before you go any farther, let the Father catch you and bring restoration. He's waiting, and watching. By the way, He's a long distance runner, and He always wins.

How come some are so cold, sour and hardened? Maybe because they haven't received or given daily grace. The older boy tells his father that he had never been given a goat. Maybe you have never dealt with a goat, but most are very stubborn and obstinate.

While I was pastoring my first church, someone dropped off two goats. Quickly, I made a few calls, and found a so-called goat man. (That's what everyone called him, no kidding.) He comes to get them; the first one wasn't any trouble at all. He seemed to enjoy boarding a trailer. However, the other goat wouldn't cooperate. With his long sharp horns he would charge at the goat man.

This goat had made up his mind, he owned the place, and no one, not even God was welcome. (Sound like someone you know?)

The goat man finally gave up, and drove off, seemingly beaten by the tough mean animal.

For the next three days, no one could get near him. Several more want-a-be goat men tried taking this stubborn ugly goat home. As his next victim walked toward him, this goat's pupils seem to dilate while he peeled his eyes right through them. If they made any sudden moves toward him, he would begin to walk closer and dare them.

He stayed outside right next to our double doors in the front entrance of the church. I can remember feeling the hair on the back of my neck stand up as I looked at the goat. No kidding, this was no ordinary goat. He seemed to own the church building, and no one challenged him on his decision.

I truly was convinced this goat was possessed by the devil himself. Finally I'd had enough, so I took care of that old goat. I'll never tell you what happened to him, lets just say, he disappeared.

Going back to the older brother, he asked for a goat, and he had the mentality of a goat. However, his father was cooking a lamb. Again, goats are obstinate, while lambs are gentle and easily led.

Usually, a person speaks what is in his or her heart. I believe this brother had a goat mentality. He was stubborn, and set in his ways. He had become very presumptuous and too familiar with his surroundings and family. He took them and his life for granted. In other words, he took advantage of his father's house. He lost total respect for his father, so his father was nothing more than an old familiar object that stayed in his way all the time.

However, just like the oldest son, many in the body of Christ need an attitude adjustment, or maybe even a drastic change in scenery.

Jesus said, In My Father's house... (John 14,1) This son didn't realize what was in his Father's house. His imagination had shut down, even though his surroundings were picturesque all he saw was gloom and doom. Again, he took his father for granted. Maybe his attitude was, *"Father is around, and I have no worries."* He became too familiar, His movement, ways and actions were now normal.

Nothing his father accomplished fazed him. Bills were paid, groceries on the table, and a place to lay his head.

All the same, there are people in the body of Christ that take Father God for granted. He longs to perform miracles, heal, give gifts unto men, and pour favor out onto them, but they have limited the very 'One' who could bring drastic change.

However, for many people like this older brother, none of this is recognized or appreciated. An unrepentant heart is unable to be grateful. God gave only one formula for all to come to Him and I should mention He's speaking this word to believers today, *If My people who are called by My name will humble themselves, and pray and seek My face, and turn from their wicked ways, then I will hear from heaven, and will forgive their sin and* heal their land.[6]

But as soon as this son of yours came, who has devoured your livelihood with harlots, you killed the fatted calf for him.[7] Notice the language, "this son of yours..."

"The sad fact is many pastors and leaders spend too much time trying to win over an offended individual."

You've heard the phrase, hurting people, hurt people. Someone with a low self-esteem starts off by needing approval. However, they never find gratification, so later he or she withdraws and acts as though no one is needed.

This boy is hurting and everyone will pay. What should be done for the older brother? If he's not confronted, there's little anyone can do. His attitude has to be addressed, he cannot be allowed to treat others anyway he chooses. If there isn't any change, further action should transpire.

No one can be allowed to manipulate by his or her sour actions, and bitter fruit.

By experience, I can tell you, if this *older brother spirit* isn't addressed and dealt with, it will discourage others, and they will follow this route. Discipline isn't fun, but it has to be done.

Sometimes, discipline is grace in action. If all options have been exhausted it leaves no other alternative but to bring uncomfortable actions. Once again, leaving the ninety-nine, and saving the one sounds good in theory; but sometimes, punishing the one, for the sake of the ninety-nine is the only answer that brings results.

This kind of punishment has a two-fold effect. First, for the oldest sons sake, and secondly for the hire-hands sake. They will forever have this in their memory, *"hey you know what, if I mess up there will be repercussions."*

This boy is quick to point out his brother's sins, and he even names them. However, hear his fathers response, *"And he said to him, 'Son, you are always with me, and all that I have is yours. It was right that we should make merry and be glad, for your brother was dead and is alive again, and was lost and is found."*[8] Mankind can have money in the bank and everything else under the sun; however, if he or she doesn't have grace they have nothing.

A blank stare is normal; substances can never replace the God spot of every human. Surfing the Internet, sports, games or material goods can't bring fulfillment. Again, when our relationship with Christ is void, nothing satisfies, even while living in the Father's house.

Look at this last verse with me again, the father speaking to his older son, ...*It was right that we should make merry and be glad, for your brother was dead and is alive again, and was lost and is found.'*

The older brother might have been experiencing the latest phenomenon growing out of control around the world, especially here in America called, *Anhedonia*. It refers to the reduced ability to experience pleasure. *"Scientists are adamant that as we push the stress level and exciting stimulation higher and higher, we are literally overloading the pathways to the pleasure center of the brain. This overload causes our brain's pleasure center to demand a further increase in the level of stimulation before delivering more feeling of pleasure. This results in a decline in our pleasure system's ability to deliver enjoyment out of ordinary, simple things."*[9]

Millions wake every morning with no meaning, or purpose even though they have everything money can buy. Hear me, money won't replace the simple pleasures of God and family.

This older boy was caught in a trap. He was self-centered, with a larger than life ego. He was driven within, and close to collapse. No one met his unrealistic standards, not even himself. Now, without a heart change, he was poised to make others miserable with him.

The good news is God's grace is available, all someone needs to do is ask. So what are you waiting for? As the story ends in Luke 15, these two young men are brothers in name only but thankfully God's grace is still available.

This grace that can save, is unfathomable. We will never understand it because it hasn't come from this world. *That's why the last verse in the hymn, Amazing Grace says, "When we've been there ten thousand years, bright shinning as the sun; We've no less days to sing God's praise, than when we first begun."*[10]

Questions
Can be answered in a group, or as an individual

Do you get along with your siblings?

Recently has anyone shown grace and love to you?

Do you know of any old goats? (People) How do you deal with them?

Do you have grace, and do you show grace to others?

What's some prayer request you need people to agreement with?

Chapter 6
Kingdom Authority

Then the seventy returned with joy, saying, "Lord, even the demons are subject to us in Your name."

And He said to them, "I saw Satan fall like lightning from heaven. Behold, I give you the authority to trample on serpents and scorpions, and over all the power of the enemy, and nothing shall by any means hurt you. Nevertheless do not rejoice in this, that the spirits are subject to you, but rather rejoice because your names are written in heaven."

Luke 10:17-20 NKJ

Jesus' disciples were on a mission, but for how long they had been gone isn't known, possibly several weeks. As they returned the disciples report was, *"demons are subject to the name of Jesus."* The prophet Isaiah reminds his audience of satan's upheaval and demise.

"How you are fallen from heaven, O Lucifer, son of the morning! How you are cut down to the ground, You who weakened the nations! For you have said in your heart: I will ascend into heaven, I will exalt my throne above the stars of God; I will also sit on the mount of the congregation On the farthest sides of the north; I will ascend above the heights of the clouds, I will be like the Most High.' Yet you shall be brought down to Sheol, To the lowest depths of the Pit. " Those who see you will gaze at you, And consider you, saying:' Is this the man who made the earth tremble, Who shook kingdoms,[1]

Jesus' rebuttal was, *"don't be surprised that demons are subject to you."* However Jesus made sure His disciples understood that He had watched this fallen angel, called satan, cast from heaven.

This is important because every believer needs to understand his or her rights, and authority as a faithful wittiness for the Lord.

Again Jesus' disciples came back with excitement, *"Lord, even the demons are subject to us in Your name."* What's in Jesus' name? *All power and authority.*

Authority is delegated power. In Greek power means dynamis authority exousia. We have delegated authority. Delegated authority implies that we don't have this authority in our self, but that another gives it to us. We therefore don't stand forth on our own behalf, but on behalf of another.[2]

"Authority is delegated power"

Authority grants power, or right delegated or given; authorization: A person or body of persons in whom authority is vested, as a governmental agency. Usually, authorities. Persons having the legal power to make and enforce the law; government.[3]

Of course, this terminology is given for a democratic society; however, He alone rules His kingdom- it's that simple.

Therefore if you live by faith, it's time to start activating God's authority through your person. You have the Mighty God living within; it's not about how you feel. It's all about you taking authority over everything by faith.

In late December while at the gym I was on the treadmill going my usual two-miles. The man beside me was doing the same; however, he had on a sweatshirt, a hood, and another heavy-duty shirt along with two pair of thick paints.

He was trying to change his outward appearance with outward gear; unfortunately, it won't work. Just as change starts within for the physical; change begins within for those who believe.

Before authority can come to and flow through any believer, he or she must allow faith to override every circumstance and emotion. The truth is, *that if you confess with your mouth the Lord Jesus and believe in your heart that God has raised Him from the dead, you will be saved. For with the heart one believes unto righteousness, and with the mouth confession is made unto salvation. For the Scripture says, "Whoever believes on Him will not be put to shame."*[4]

Would you agree with me when salvation entered, eternity came into full view? Therefore, salvation changes everything, and because you agree with me, everything else pertaining to God's word is yours also.

The measure of faith that has been given you is meant for growth and development. You are now wired to grow in Christ and even reproduce.

With your new belief system in tact you can take authority over, and even lay hands on anyone who needs transformation. You are now God's agent; you work, act and speak for God.

Several times a week I will look at my hands and speak over them. *"Hands you are anointed to do God's work. You were created by God, and I declare my hands and fingers to be filled with faith, healing and miracles."*

These adjectives for Christ are rather long, but I feel its important you understand what Christ has accomplished for you. Jesus Christ is... He's Advocate (1 John 2:1) Almighty (Rev. 1:8; Mt. 28:18)

Alpha and Omega (Rev. 1:8; 22:13)

Jesus Christ is... Amen (Rev. 3:14)

He's the... Apostle of our Profession (Heb. 3:1)

Atoning Sacrifice for our Sins (1 John 2:2)

Author of Life (Acts 3:15)

Author and Perfecter of our Faith (Heb. 12:2)

Author of Salvation (Heb. 2:10)

Beginning and End (Rev. 22:13) Blessed and only Ruler (1 Tim. 6:15)

Bread of God (John 6:33) Bread of Life (John 6:35; 6:48)

Bridegroom (Mt. 9:15)

Capstone (Acts 4:11; 1 Pet. 2:7)

Chief Cornerstone (Eph. 2:20)

Chief Shepherd (1 Pet. 5:4)

Jesus Christ is... Christ (1 John 2:22)

Creator (John 1:3)

Deliverer (Rom. 11:26) Eternal Life (1 John 1:2; 5:20)

Gate (John 10:9)

Faithful and True (Rev. 19:11)

Faithful Witness (Rev. 1:5)

Faith and True Witness (Rev. 3:14)

First and Last (Rev. 1:17; 2:8; 22:13)

He the... Firstborn From the Dead (Rev. 1:5)

Firstborn over all creation (Col. 1:15)

Gate (John 10:9)

Jesus Christ is... God (John 1:1; 20:28; Heb. 1:8; Rom. 9:5)

Good Shepherd (John 10:11,14) Great Shepherd (Heb. 13:20)

Great High Priest (Heb. 4:14)

Head of the Church (Eph. 1:22; 4:15; 5:23)

Heir of all things (Heb. 1:2)

High Priest (Heb. 2:17)

Holy and True (Rev. 3:7) Holy One (Acts 3:14)

Hope (1 Tim. 1:1)

Hope of Glory (Col. 1:27)

Horn of Salvation (Luke 1:69)

Jesus Christ is... I Am (John 8:58)

He's the... Image of God (2 Cor. 4:4)

Immanuel (Mt. 1:23)

Judge of the living and the dead (Acts 10:42)

King Eternal (1 Tim. 1:17)

King of Israel (John 1:49)

King of the Jews (Mt. 27:11)

King of kings (1 Tim 6:15; Rev. 19:16)

King of the Ages (Rev. 15:3)

Lamb (Rev. 13:8)

Lamb of God (John 1:29)

Lamb Without Blemish (1 Pet. 1:19)

Last Adam (1 Cor. 15:45)

Life (John 14:6; Col. 3:4)

Light of the World (John 8:12)

Lion of the Tribe of Judah (Rev. 5:5)
Living One (Rev. 1:18)
Living Stone (1 Pet. 2:4)
Lord (2 Pet. 2:20)
Jesus Christ is... Lord of All (Acts 10:36)
Lord of Glory (1 Cor. 2:8)
Lord of lords (Rev. 19:16)
Man from Heaven (1 Cor. 15:48)
Mediator of the New Covenant (Heb. 9:15)
Mighty God (Isa. 9:6)
Morning Star (Rev. 22:16)
Offspring of David (Rev. 22:16)
Only Begotten Son of God (John 1:18; 1 John 4:9)
Our Great God and Savior (Titus 2:13)
Our Holiness (1 Cor. 1:30)
Our Husband (2 Cor. 11:2)
Our Protection (2 Thess. 3:3)
Our Redemption (1 Cor. 1:30)
Our Righteousness (1 Cor. 1:30)
Our Sacrificed Passover Lamb (1 Cor. 5:7)
Power of God (1 Cor. 1:24)Precious Cornerstone (1 Pet. 2:6)
Prophet (Acts 3:22)
Rabbi (Mt. 26:25)
Resurrection and Life (John 11:25)
Righteous Branch (Jer. 23:5)

Righteous One (Acts 7:52; 1 John 2:1)

Rock (1 Cor. 10:4)

Root of David (Rev. 5:5; 22:16)

Ruler of God's Creation (Rev. 3:14) Ruler of the Kings of the Earth (Rev. 1:5)

Savior (Eph. 5:23; Titus 1:4; 3:6; 2 Pet. 2:20)

Son of David (Lk. 18:39)

Son of God (John 1:49; Heb. 4:14)

Son of Man (Mt. 8:20)

Son of the Most High God (Lk. 1:32) Source of Eternal Salvation for believers (Heb. 5:9)

The One Mediator (1 Tim. 2:5)

The Stone the builders rejected (Acts 4:11)

True Bread (John 6:32)

True Light (John 1:9)

True Vine (John 15:1)

Truth (John 1:14; 14:6)

Way (John 14:6)

Wisdom of God (1 Cor. 1:24)

Word (John 1:1)

Jesus Christ is... the Word of God. Rev. 19:13 [5]

Even though you might have been tempted just to skim over these names, I want you to understand that throughout the sixty-six books of God's word, He's available for anyone that will trust Him. Faith is believing and confessing that God's kingdom lives within you. Moreover, the same God who knew Adam and Eve as they hid in the garden of Eden naked and ashamed, knows where you are and He cares.

"Authority begins as you operate by faith; Faith is the key that unlocks every door."

While conducting a service, back in 1993, I proceeded to receive the tithe and offering. As I began sharing an appropriate scripture, a man seated in the back of the church, shouted out, *"I don't believe in anyone who collects offerings!"* I stopped dead in my tracks. It's so easy to take those procedures for granted, but suddenly, I was at a loss for words. Then the Holy Spirit prompted me to go back where he was sitting. As I did, I asked him his name and where he was from? As he opened his mouth, I could smell rank alcohol coming from his breath and even his body. I asked him if he would come to the altar with me, but he began to give me excuses. Finally, he consented. Suddenly, it was as though he desired prayer.

As I began to pray, and take authority, the man became violent. Everyone in the building cleared out of the way. Finally, he fell to the floor and I knelt beside him. I was still commanding satan to come out and trying to stand my ground. Nothing happened.

To my surprise, one of the quietest ladies in the church shouted, *"Pastor Howard, not in the name of Jesus, but **In The Name Of Jesus!**"* I had said these same words, but as she said them it was like you could feel authority coming from her small frame. I learned something that day about spiritual authority and how important it is .

This man jumped up, off the floor while I was still praying for him fervently. Let me just say, *"This wasn't fun, nor would I desire anyone having to do this; however, at the same time it's what our world needs."* To make a long story short, I will tell you this man was set free. No longer bound by satan, to God be the glory!

Hear Jesus' words unto His disciples. *See what I've given you? Safe passage as you walk on snakes and scorpions, and protection from every assault of the Enemy. No one can put a hand on you.*[6] The authority you walk in, as a believer, is for certain and it has been entrusted to you.

Satan's biggest threat comes when you find out who you are, and whose you are. If authority is taken for granted, or is misused, you become the foolish one. However, if you will consent to becoming an ambassador for Jesus Christ, He will take your life and you will be forever changed.

There are too many believers that want blessings without a price, and no commitment. Authority isn't about being a spiritual giant. It doesn't mean you won't have difficult times that come and go; but you will realize whose you are, and that you have a higher calling and purpose for life.

"This is the fact; you have greater authority as a child of the king than any single person walking in any government position including the president of the United States. As you walk in the Lord Jesus Christ, by faith, you become a force to be reckoned with. As you live, speak, and do, you function as a representative of a

king. Jesus Christ is your elder brother. He has given you His rights and privileges. You are called Sons and Daughter of God."

As I walk, I am focused on my king; therefore, as He gives me His plan, I try my best to follow it through. Back in 2005, I heard the Lord as He gave me another assignment; first, I had a call from my overseer asking me to consider another church he felt I could help.

As Jenny and I were in prayer to consider this new assignment, she quickly glanced out our back window. Behind our house we had a pond, and on the banks, from out of nowhere, was a very large bird, just standing there. *"Sounds funny, and really it was!" We had never seen a bird like this, ever. It was a crane in our back yard! Jenny and I have been married for 25 years, and this was a first.* It would have just been a real attention grabber, right? But, the name of the church we were to pray about has a very unusual name: Crane Eater Community Church.

Now listen closely, I am not into fleeces, nor do I trust or look for them. Fleeces are of the

Old Testament but faith today is of the New Covenant. God has a wonderful sense of humor however, and I believe He allowed that Crane to fly into our back yard that day, just to give us a sense of His control. The assignment given to us hasn't been without difficulty, but walking by faith is what God wants us all to do. With the help of the Lord, along with great men and women of God, we have been able to grow, and build a new worship facility right in the middle of the worse economy in years.

"Authority gives you passion mixed with faith that will speak and follow through."

What happens when you don't understand your authority? Well let's look at a real story in the book of Acts. *A group of Jews was traveling from town to town casting out evil spirits. They tried to use the name of the Lord Jesus in their incantation, saying, "I command you in the name of Jesus, whom Paul preaches, to come out!" Seven sons of Sceva, a leading priest, were doing this. But one time when they tried it, the evil spirit replied, "I know Jesus, and I know Paul, but who are you?" Then the man with the evil spirit leaped on them, overpowered them, and attacked them with such violence that they fled from the house, naked and battered.*[7]

◆They traveled from town to town- this tells me they had no covering; no spiritual head or mentor.

◆They used the name of Jesus as a ploy, and even as part of their incantation or charm to gain fame.

◆ Because of no spiritual covering; they did what they wanted to do, and followed their own rules and guidelines.

◆They didn't have a personal relationship with Jesus Christ.

◆These Jews tried to mimic what Paul unselfishly did to help others.

◆The evil spirits knew these men had no authority, and leaped upon them, overpowered, and attacked them with such violence that they fled from the house, naked and battered.

False or no authority brings embarrassment, and is seen by everyone, but on the other hand everyone notices Godly authority.

And Jesus came and spoke to them, saying, *"All authority has been given to Me in heaven and on earth. Go therefore and make disciples of all the nations, baptizing them in the name of the Father and of the Son and of the Holy Spirit, teaching them to observe all things that I have commanded you; and lo, I am with you always, even to the end of the age." Amen.*[8]
You have delegated authority from a king that rules His kingdom. You belong to Him; so stop portraying your king as lowly or unworthy. He's the Master Creator, and longs to be trusted, so stand up and be counted as a kingdom heir.

Paul explores the contracts between the condemning act of Adam and the redemptive act of Christ. Adam's sin brought universal death- satan promised Adam, *"you will be like God."* He lied. However, Jesus' sacrifice brought salvation to those who believe. Again, now you are sons and daughters of God. *"Remember this, Jesus' one act of redemption was immeasurably greater than Adam's one act of condemnation."*

Romans 5:17b...much more those who receive abundance of grace and of the gift of righteousness will reign in life through the One, Jesus Christ.

Abundance of grace, *"how much is that?" Did I get just enough to get by and that's it? Or maybe just a teacup full, or a measure of grace? Or how about just enough to get saved and no more, is that all the grace that God extended to me, and now am I on my own?*

It is abundant; it is given without a hitch, without strings attached and without measurement. It keeps on giving every moment of every day, throughout our entire lives. Unlike Adam's act, Christ's act has, and will accomplish exactly what He intended. He's called us to reign!

That's a period during which something or somebody is dominant or powerful. The word reign here means to reign in life as a king, to have kingly rule and to possess kingly dominion. Based on the authority of God's Word, you are destined to "reign in life" as a king, to have kingly dominion over all your challenges and circumstances.

You are called to be above them all, and not be trampled by them.

"The time has come for you to stop abdicating your right to reign in life."

Remember, God through His Son has positioned you and called you for such a time as this.

While in one of my seminary classes I had a full semester on these eight verses. Therefore I declare over you, and every person whom you will be willing to speak these words over, they will be truly blessed.

"If you fully obey the Lord your God and carefully keep all his commands that I am giving you today, the Lord your God will set you high above all the nations of the world. You will experience all these blessings if you obey the Lord your God: Your towns and your fields will be blessed. Your children and your crops will be blessed. The offspring of your herds and flocks will be blessed. Your fruit baskets and breadboards will be blessed. Wherever you go and whatever you do, you will be blessed. "The Lord will conquer your enemies when they attack you. They will attack you from one direction, but they will scatter from you in seven! "The Lord will guarantee a blessing on everything you do and will fill your storehouses with grain. The Lord your God will bless you in the land he is giving you."[8]

Daily decide to declare the blessings of God over you, and your family. It will make a difference and even bring wonderful breakthroughs for everyone you declare as blessed.

Questions
Can be answered in a group, or as an individual

Do you walk with spiritual authority?

By faith, do you speak to mountains?

What are your mountains?

Do you have a spiritual covering?

Do you know your church leaders?

Do you have knowledge of your purpose with the body of Christ?

Chapter 7

Provision

*Now Elijah, who was from Tishbe in Gilead,
told King Ahab, "As surely as the Lord, the
God of Israel, lives—the God I serve—there
will be no dew or rain during the next few
years until I give the word!" Then the Lord
said to Elijah, "Go to the east and hide by
Kerith Brook, near where it enters the Jordan
River. Drink from the brook and eat what the
ravens bring you, for I have commanded them
to bring you food." So Elijah did as the Lord
told him and camped beside Kerith Brook,
east of the Jordan. The ravens brought him
bread and meat each morning and evening,
and he drank from the brook. But after a
while the brook dried up, for there was no
rainfall anywhere in the land.*

I Kings 17:1-7 NKJ

I couldn't begin to inform you on how many times God has proven Himself faithful to me, and as far as that goes to all believer's that trust Him.

Notice before the prophet could go any further he had to confront his enemy. He had to meet his adversary and speak the truth. Also notice Elijah doesn't share God's plans with Ahab. He simply shares how God will change nature to interrupt the enemy's plans.

Elijah's name means, "The Lord is God." Elijah's ministry corresponded to his name: He was sent from God to confront Baalism and to declare to Israel that the Lord was God and there was no other.[1]

You also have been created by the Master to make a difference. To change the world around you. It might start with your neighborhood, or maybe your community.

God spoke through this one man, and said, *"As the Lord God lives, and it will not rain for 3 ½ years."* Of course, this was a tall order and would affect the just and the unjust.

However, God spoke to Elijah and directed his path. While others suffered, Elijah received provision from God Himself.

Trust in the LORD with all your heart, And lean not on your own understanding; In all your ways acknowledge Him, And He shall direct[your paths.²

Think for a moment, imagine that there are no spring rains and the ponds and lakes are all dried up. No dew on the ground, everything chapped and dusty. This drought proved that Baal, the god of the rains and fertility, was impotent before the Lord.

Remember this simple word:

"If God doesn't provide, it won't be fruitful or eternal."

Do you really desire what God hasn't endorsed? The approval of God means provision, and it's just a matter of time before He will be glorified. *Let God arise, Let His enemies be scattered; Let those also who hate Him flee before Him.³*

"Provision without vision won't last."

You might want to write that down because it's truth. Provision will manifest as someone operates by faith. The seed you have in your hands is for sowing. Remember the young lads lunch in the gospels became the seed that fed 5,000- as he placed His lunch in the Master's hands.

The provision you need comes from the same source- Jesus Christ. Why not begin to profess by faith what you need before the Mighty God, Jehovah.

Provision also begins with your faith statement. *"As surely as the Lord, the God of Israel, lives—the God I serve...* No one can teach this, or drill this into you. Jesus has to become your complete faith constitution. It's not just you speaking faith; it's you living faith. What you talk, is what you will walk and vice-versa.

Elijah is saying, "He lives in me, and I hear and know His voice." Hear what Elijah harkens unto Ahab- *"there will be no dew or rain during the next few years until I give the word!"* When a believer begins to speak with this type of authority, God will hear their words!

This kind of faith moves mountains! Mountains of debt, relationships, or anything else becomes just a drop in the bucket. No it's not hocus-pocus, its real genuine faith that endures even hardships.

Say this with genuine authority, *"Provision come!"*

'The silver is Mine, and the gold is Mine,' says the LORD of hosts.⁴
Then the Lord said to Elijah, "Go to the east and hide by Kerith Brook, near where it enters the Jordan River. Drink from the brook and eat what the ravens bring you, for I have commanded them to bring you food."⁵

Provision came because Elijah followed God faithfully through the dry times (no pun intended).

I have been senior pastor for over 20 years now, and I have watched faithful followers leave this world rejoicing- that's provision.

Back in 1990, the Lord prompted me to begin helping a needy woman by giving her a ride to church. She lived with a disability in her spine and neck that left her wearing a brace; however, even with her brace it had to be specially built because of the deep curve in her neck.

She was very grateful for the ride, and began to show deep spiritual growth inwardly as well as her outward actions. To say the least, she became a weekly joy that Jenny and I looked forward to. As the months followed, she told me she was looking for a settlement for her years of suffering, and when she received it she felt lead to give my family a love gift for helping her. Of course, Jenny and I never mentioned this to her and thought she was just trying to show appreciation to us for picking her up.

Come to find out she had worked for the same company for over 30 years as a telemarketer with an old fashion phone closely propped up to her neck, and ear. Developing over those years of work was a painful curve in her spine. To be blunt, her continual pain was persistent and getting worse.

I always believed with her for a miracle, and by God's grace, the daily pain never dampened her spirit.

Finally one month she told me she was going to be moving away. The whole church family was saddened.

About one year after her move, she called Jenny and I to ask if we could come see her. We set up a time and made a road trip to her house. As we entered her modest home, there she was sitting at her kitchen table, and next to her was an old cassette player. She invited us to sit down, and as we did she popped in a tape. As we listened to the song *"Thank You For Giving to The Lord,"* we all wept openly. Suddenly, she reached into her pocket and pulled out a folded envelope and said, "Please accept this love offering, Pastor Howard. I have to obey the Lord". It was so heart humbling to receive this precious woman's gift.

The fact is, she was the poorest woman in our church and yet she stayed true to the promise she had made to God.

Would this have happened if there had been wrong motives on our part or hers? I think not. This one lady made it possible for God's provision to come our way, and help us to continue in His plan so we could help others.

"God used the poorest woman in our church"

Right now may I pray a simple blessing over you?

"May peace break into your home and may abundance come and steal your debts. May the pockets of your jeans become a magnet for God's provision. May love stick to your face like honey and may laughter assault your lips! May happiness come across your face and may your tears be that of joy. May the problems you had, forget your home address."

"Don't even think about telling me God doesn't bring provision!"

So Elijah did as the Lord told him and camped beside Kerith Brook, east of the Jordan. The ravens brought him bread and meat each morning and evening, and he drank from the brook.[6]

Naturally speaking, the river Jordan and Ravens? First, the Jordan isn't known for the purest looking water, but God provided. Secondly, ravens are in the same species as the black bird, and for some odd reason this just doesn't turn my appetite on, but once again God provided.

Remember this fact, provision might not come the way you think it should come, but God's way will ultimately bring the best outcome.

Notice Elijah camped or stayed near the brook. In other words he didn't get bored, or tire of God's provisions. The prophet camped out with God being Johavah-Jirah. (The Lord is my provider.)

I've known great men of God with a strong call on their life that wouldn't leave their security and totally trust in God's provision; therefore, he or she never experienced God's best. They never could fulfill or be trusted with a full place or position in ministry.

I submit to you that all God desires is a *"Yes, I will follow."* One more point I might add, provision isn't glamorous- it's just walking faithfully.

But after a while the brook dried up, for there was no rainfall anywhere in the land.

Finally, remember the provision God makes for you can change, so by all means follow His direction. Don't become stubborn, or stay somewhere for the sake of staying; follow God and stay cheerful.

"You can be sure that God will take care of everything you need, his generosity exceeding even yours in the glory that pours from Jesus."[7]

"Beware of these teachers of religious law! For they like to parade around in flowing robes and receive respectful greetings as they walk in the marketplaces. And how they love the seats of honor in the synagogues and the head table at banquets. Yet they shamelessly cheat widows out of their property and then pretend to be pious by making long prayers in public. Because of this, they will be more severely punished."[8] Read closely the next few verses and then I would like to shed some light on these verses.

Jesus sat down near the collection box in the Temple and watched as the crowds dropped in their money. Many rich people put in large amounts. Then a poor widow came and dropped in two small coins. Jesus called his disciples to him and said, "I tell you the truth, this poor widow has given more than all the others who are making contributions. For they gave a tiny part of their surplus, but she, *poor as she is, has given everything she had to live on."*⁹

Jesus exposed the greedy practices of some scribes. Scribes often served as estate planners for widows, which gave them the opportunity to convince distraught widows out of their money. These scribes effectively robbed the widow of her husband's legacy.

"Could this widow be one of those widows who were robbed by the scribes Jesus mentions in verses 38-40?"

This widow gives her whole livelihood. I believe she understood that her means wouldn't come unless it came supernaturally.

While looking at these verses I should point out that I just read you this in its context.

As you read scripture you will notice, many times it was the widow who listened.

Almost everyone is familiar with the name Corrie ten Boom, but her brother also was a great man of God who walked in God's provision. *Peter just a young boy when he set out to save hundreds of baby's from the concentration camps and certain death. At least 40 some years later Peter was on a journey to Israel teaching and giving testimony for the gospel of Christ when suddenly he suffered a heart attack. After determination was made that Peter's body required open-heart surgery the on call doctor read his name on the surgery list, ask him was he related to Corrie ten Boom? Peter replied, "Yes she's my sister." The doctor wept and replied, "I am one of the babies you saved!" After Peter's recovery he thanked the doctor, but of course his physician rebuttal, "You saved my life as an infant, so now I saved your life."[10]*

Here are just a few names for God that you should learn throughout your journey of faith and provision.

El Shaddai: (Gen 17:1) The All Sufficient One / Almighty God
El Elyon: (Gen 14:18-20) The Most High God
Adonai: (Is 6:8) Our Master
Jehovah: (Ex 3:14) The Lord of the already, right now, and not yet (past/present/future)

Jehovah-Nissi: (Ex 17:15) The Lord our Banner and Battle Ax

Jehovah-Rohi: (Ps 23) The Lord our Shepherd

Jehovah-Rapha: (Ex 15:26) The Lord our Healer

Jehovah-Shammah: (Eze 48:35) The Lord that is Present with us

Jehovah-Tsidkenu: (Jer 23:6) The Lord that makes us Righteous

Jehovah-M'kaddesh: (Lev 20:8) The Lord that Sets us Apart

Jehovah-Jireh: (Gen 22:14) The Lord our Provider

Jehovah-Shalom: (Jud 6:24) The Lord our Peace

Jehovah-Sabaoth: (1 Sam 1:3) The Lord of all Armies

El Olam: (Is 26:4) The Lord that lasts Forever

El Gibhor: (Ps 24:8) The Mighty God

El Roi: (Gen 16:13) The Lord that Sees us in Every Situation

Elohim: (Gen 1:1) Our Creative God [11]

Bringing to remembrance the names of God can actually help you grow personally in times of need. *But recall the former days in which, after you were illuminated, you endured a great struggle with sufferings.*[12] Truly God wants to become the Jehovah-Jireh for you, so relinquish every care and worry over to Him and you my friend will have a head start.

A blessing spoken over Crane Eater Community Church, by Bishop Dale C. Bronner. He's the Senior pastor Word of Faith Family Worship Cathedral in Atlanta Georgia with over 18,000 members.

"I pray God's blessings on Crane Eater for 2011, that great anointing and power will flow!

May there be people drawn there from every direction! May the music be celestial and may the Word transform the mindsets of the people.

May 2011 be your best year thus far at Crane Eater. The best is yet to come!

I hear the sound of the ABUNDANCE of rain for your ministry this year!

God does not send rain where there is no seed sown. You've been faithful to sow seed, and now God will abundantly send rain. Get ready! Get ready! Get ready!

Your borders of influence and blessings are about to expand. Blessings to you, my friend."

Questions
Can be answered in a group, or as an individual

What provisions has God definitely made for you?

Daily, do you trust God?

How do you feel about blessing someone who has blessed you?

Do you believe you can hear the voice of God?

Are you obedient unto the voice of God? Do you think God care how you give?

Do you tithe? / Give offerings?

Chapter 8

The Holy Spirit And His Help

Likewise the Spirit also helps in our weaknesses. For we do not know what we should pray for as we ought, but the Spirit Himself makes intercession for us with groanings which cannot be uttered. Now He who searches the hearts knows what the mind of the Spirit is, because He makes intercession for the saints according to the will of God.

Romans 8:26-27 NKJ

The Holy Spirit can become your best friend and helper, it's that simple. He desires to help you through your daily walk. He's the One who Jesus said, He would pray, and ask His Father to send when He (Jesus) left, and that He would abide with you forever.

The Holy Spirit has many facets, one being our comforter. A comforter relieves stress and worry while replacing these slow grinding killers with rest and peace in the midst of a storm.

Back in 1988, I was a life insurance agent for a debit company. My job was to go door-to-door collecting on monthly or weekly insurance policies. This is where I grew in the Lord; this is the place I learned,first hand, about the pain of humanity, and their deep need for Christ. The Lord truly used this experience to hewn out His calling in me.

One summer afternoon I was on my route while suddenly a forceful storm came out of nowhere. I left the last apartment with an elderly lady pleading with me to stay until the storm passed because she was worried for my safety . I actually left her house to go back to my small pickup truck to pray and read God's word.

As I was sitting in my truck, the wind picked up speed to the point of moving the tail end of my vehicle up and down.

However, the wonderful presence of the Holy Spirit was evident while I was sitting there. No fear or worry bothered me. In fact, just the opposite, peace and joy in the Holy Ghost filled that small truck. Why is that important?

Now I'm not saying to go and stand in the eye of a storm to test your peace level; but I am testifying that if you need Him, He will be there. The Holy Spirit will guide you and bring powerful comfort and joy in the midst of any situation.

Paul writes that the Spirit helps in our weaknesses. We all know that every individual on the planet deals with frailties and problems. The Spirit can help equip, and bring stability in the middle of any situation in your life.

Here's a powerful key to remember and practice; the Holy Spirit loves to be invited and welcomed into your everyday life.

"The Spirit can help equip, and bring stability in the middle of any situation in your life."

As a chaplain I can't tell you how many times the Spirit of God has brought peace in the midst of calamity. I have personally seen the effects of tragedy unfold, yet the Holy Spirit brought comfort. He was there with a peaceful bridge of calm, even though pain and sorrow was all around.

Back in 2003, while traveling back and forth to seminary, driving around a curve on a two lane county road, I came upon a terrible accident. First, I noticed the smoking wreckage of a large van and it looked as though it was about to catch on fire. Secondly, I saw a young man trapped in a demolished car that had been flattened. It actually seemed as though the young man was going in, and out of consciousness. I quickly ran and cut the engine off of the smoldering van, and then proceeded to go back to the young man trapped in the car.

What I failed to tell you is how shaken and terrified I was. There was no help for this young man except for me and I knew I couldn't offer medical assistance.

Suddenly, the Holy Spirit came upon me to bring direction. The Lord gave me holy boldness with words of comfort and peace. I was able to lead this young man to Jesus. Finally, emergency vehicles came and immediately went to work to stabilize him. Realizing everything was under control, I traveled on to school in awe of the God of Peace. What happened Howard? The Holy Spirit arrived.

*And I will ask the Father, and He will give you another Comforter **(Counselor, Helper, Intercessor, Advocate, Strengthener, and Standby)**, that He <u>may remain with you forever</u>*—[1] Please hear this plea, until Christ comes again, and receives <u>His bride,</u> (that's the body of Christ-you and I) the Holy Spirit is here to help you in every way.

Whatever you may be thinking right now, I plead with you, don't doubt the Holy Spirit, or be skeptical of His ways, unless you really know Him, and guess what? Then you will love Him and His presence.

Go back to the verse you just read and read it again, especially the adjectives highlighted in black. Because, in this one verse you will find that the Holy Spirit isn't inferior.

Meanwhile, the moment we get tired in the waiting, God's Spirit is right alongside helping us along. If we don't know how or what to pray, it doesn't matter. He does our praying in and for us, making prayer out of our wordless sighs, our aching groans.[2]

I have actually heard authentic stories of men and women who were on the mission field and other places doing God's work when suddenly, something freakish happened, a near miss or impending danger. Come to find out, someone they knew, had gathered a tremendous burden for them back home, not knowing why. They didn't know that the minister or layperson was in harms way, and in need of divine intervention.

What happened? A dear saint of God felt a terrible burden to pray at that particular time with groaning and utterances not even understood by the saint. The Holy Spirit had once again intervened!

In Mark chapter four, Jesus was fast asleep on a small boat while suddenly a huge storm came on the sea. It proceeded to hit and threatened to even sink the boat and kill everyone on board. His disciples were acting frantic. *"Where is Jesus; doesn't He care?"*

Jesus was awakened not by the storm, but by His worried disciples. He just spoke to the storm. You might say, *"Well that was Jesus!"*

Let me remind you what Jesus once said, *But* **you** *shall receive power (ability, efficiency, and might) when the Holy Spirit has come upon you, and you shall be My witnesses in Jerusalem and all Judea and Samaria and to the ends (the very bounds) of the earth.* ² Look again at the last statement in that verse. ... *And to the ends (the very bounds) of the earth.*

"That's you my friend, you are now approved to be empowered for this life and eternity to come."

Back around 1994, I was asked to preach at an outdoor church service. The Lord prompted me to preach from the book of Revelation and it was a difficult message because of the harshness of the subject. It was summer with the heat index in the high 90's that evening but under that old tin shed it seemed a lot hotter.

Surprisingly, there were quite a few people there. As I preached, the power of the Holy Spirit brought a strong anointing upon me. I knew the Lord was moving with conviction in the hearts of those who would yield to Him.

The wonderful power of the Holy Spirit, drew ten men to the altar and they were saved. That very night, three of the men left that simple meeting announcing a call on their lives. They began working in the field of ministry and one of the three entered into full-time evangelism.

When I asked James, a friend of mine, who was at the meeting that night, *"Didn't they go get any training?"* His rebuttal back was, *"Well I guess they just trusted God's word, and believed in the power of God".* The Holy Ghost is truly amazing!

So too the [Holy] Spirit comes to our aid and

bears us up in our weakness; for we do not know what prayer to offer nor how to offer it worthily as we ought, but the Spirit Himself goes to meet our supplication and pleads in our behalf with unspeakable yearnings and groanings too deep for utterance.[3] I cannot begin to tell you the many times the Holy Spirit has come to my aid, but I can say this, *on every occasion He has brought Godly wisdom with words that calmed during turmoil and peace to a tired mind.*

I have been in positions that I couldn't bear any longer and suddenly the Holy Spirit placed a great burden upon me to go somewhere and pray, or simply fall to my knees right there. It is to God's glory, that I am changed with a vision and a new hope for the future.

Back in May of 1988, after a Sunday morning service something amazing happened to me. It was at the old Cartersville Church of God, where Doctor Joe E. Edwards was then, the new pastor. I was leaving unchanged and stubborn, like I had done so many times before. Newly married and full of myself, it seemed I just couldn't serve the Lord no matter how hard I tried.

Unexpectedly, as I was walking out the front door of the sanctuary, the Holy Spirit fell upon me. Now mind you, at the time I sure didn't know, or understand anything about the Holy Spirit; I just knew something was happening to me which I had never experienced before.

I began to weep sorrowfully and realized I wasn't going anywhere. The Lord as my wittiness, I could no longer see, I just knew I had to find my wife and pray. My head fell on her shoulder as she responded to the quickening in me. Out of the 900 people attending the service that morning only three or four were still there.

Jenny immediately took me to the altar, where I fell on my knees. The few people remaining gathered around to pray as I was born again, filled with the Holy Spirit, and called to preach all in a matter of a few minutes. This was the beginning of my Spiritual life, so how could I, or would I refuse Him?

AND WHEN the day of Pentecost had fully

come, they were all assembled together in one place, When suddenly there came a sound from heaven like the rushing of a violent tempest blast, and it filled the whole house in which they were sitting. And there appeared to them tongues resembling fire, which were separated and distributed and which settled on each one of them. And they were all filled (diffused throughout their souls) with the Holy Spirit and began to speak in other (different, foreign) languages (tongues), as the Spirit kept giving them clear and loud expression [in each tongue in appropriate words].[3]

The power of Pentecost came in order to loose mankind, and to bring freedom. Pentecost is for everyone, especially for those who are tired of imitations and formality. Pentecost came to produce abundance.

Jesus intended for His disciples to be comforted, and to become confident at the same time. Pentecost is actually God's kingdom moving in, and taking control. Remember Acts 2, is for now, it's not just historical. It's the only New Testament book that doesn't have a conclusion.

Peter, a man that had miserably failed during the crucifixion of Christ, Peter, the disciple who usually spoke before he thought was a fisherman with little or no education. In spite of his faults, he bravely chose to follow the Lord's instructions and came inside the upper room that Jesus had spoken of. It was the time that all Jews came to Jerusalem to celebrate the feast of weeks (or the feast of Pentecost.) Peter was filled with emotional pain and sorrow. I don't believe that Peter, nor the other 119 followers knew just how long they would stay in that upper room. Furthermore, they weren't aware of the price they would pay for following Christ after the upper room experience. However, these men and women were desperate to carry out the words of their Jesus.

*Behold, I send the Promise of My Father upon you; but tarry in the city of Jerusalem until you are endued with power from on high."*4

Another translation says... *you will be* **clothed** *with power from on high...* This ten day act of obedience would change these 120 followers profoundly. New confidence and boldness would forever radiant from their beings.

"What the church needs today is not more or better machinery, not new organizations or more novel methods. She needs men whom the Holy Spirit can use- men of prayer, men mighty in prayer. The Holy Spirit does not flow through methods, but through men... He does not anoint plans, but men- men of prayer!" E.M. Bounds

After Jesus' promise was accomplished, and they were all filled with the Holy Spirit, Peter walked out of the upper room and heard the noise of the spectators. They were shouting, *"These men and women are all drunk and partying!"*

As Peter opened the door he proceeded to speak with new boldness that resounded into the crowd below, and 3,000 people were saved. Suddenly, their cry was, *"What must I do to be saved?"* Peter's words were, *"Repent, turn from your sins and accept Jesus Christ!"* The HolyGhost brought a new mandate, *"witness, speak and preach about Christ, and men will be saved."*

Once a failure, Peter is now the ring leader for a move of God that would sweep throughout the entire world. Furthermore, this same Spirit is still on the move today. The Holy Ghost is not limited because of your personal setbacks; He knows Jesus paid the price for your redemption in full.

As a child of the most high God you have become His son or daughter, and surly He desires you to be full until you run over.

In more recent times, men like John Wesley, Jonathan Edwards, Charles Finney, Dwight L. Moody, Charles Spurgeon, G. Campbell Morgan, R. A. Torrey, Billy Graham, and scores of other Christian leaders who have been filled with the Holy Spirit have been greatly used to further the cause of Christ and His kingdom. However, the infilling of the Holy Spirit is not limited to Christian leaders, but is available to every believer who meets God's conditions.

Hear what some of these great people of God have said about the importance of every believer experiencing the infilling of the Holy

Spirit:

Andrew Murray: *"Men ought to seek with their whole hearts to be filled with the Spirit of God. Without being filled with the Spirit, it is utterly impossible that an individual Christian or a church can ever live or work as God desires."*

Charles G. Finney: *"Christians are as guilty for not being filled with the Holy Spirit as sinners are for not repenting. They are even more so, for as they have more light, they are so much the more guilty."*

Henrietta C. Mears: *"I believe that it is impossible for any Christian to be effective either in his life or in his service unless he is filled with the Holy Spirit, who is God's only provision of power."*

Dr. J. Oswald J. Smith: *"Read the biographies of God's men and you will discover that each one sought and obtained the endowment of power from on high. One sermon preached in the anointing is worth a thousand in the energy of the flesh."*

Of course, the Holy Spirit already dwells within every believer, but obviously not every believer is filled and controlled by the Holy Spirit. But every believer can be.[5]

On January the 16th of 2011, On a Sunday morning. A young lady came to the altar for prayer. She wanted agreement about a two year old that was in a coma and bleeding from his brain as a result of an automobile accident. Christy and several from Crane Eater Community Church agreed together through prayer.

As Christy proceeded home, she received a call that this small child had come out of the coma around 12:05 and was asking for something to eat. It was exactly the same time Christy felt this need to intercede for the child while others agreed!

Melea testifies, "Around a year ago in July, my grandmother asked me if I knew someone named Josh?" I replied, "No I don't know anyone with that name beside my two cousins." She said, "No, this Josh has dark hair." She said, "Melea, there is a Josh out there for you, and he is going to be the one." "Wow, God gave my grandmother this vision of a dark haired guy named, Josh that would be in my life."

"On Saturday January the 22, 2011 I met a

dark haired guy named Josh. We have been texting and talking on the phone daily. We will be meeting each other next Saturday, February the 11th. God's truly amazing how He works, I tried to find a guy on my own, but it didn't lead me anywhere except heartbreak. I gave up, and let God take control suddenly, this amazing guy shows up."

On Sunday, January 23rd I had been teaching and preaching on abundance for the new year, 2011. After the Sunday AM service we had a committal ceremony, where we buried inscriptions representing all of our past mistakes and sorrows. I held an elderly lady's hand to help her walk outside for this service. While walking, she told me that her husband had an incurable type of cancer, and she wanted to commit this unto the Lord. After the service, our youth pastor, Larry went on my behalf to pray for her husband. Due to a prior obligation I was unable to go. Strong prayer mixed with agreement while confessing the healing power of God occurred. Mary's husband Ray, felt a tingling sensation go through his body. Encouraged by the Spirit of God, he's confessing and believing he is healed!

Remember, the Holy Spirit prays and works on your behalf; He's for you, and He never sleeps or slumbers.

I could share testimony after testimony. *And there are also many other things that Jesus did, which if they were written one by one, I suppose that even the world itself could not contain the books that would be written. Amen.*[6]

Want to know the essence of putting your faith into action? It's simple: Act the way you want to be, and soon you'll be the way you act! [7]

"That's the power of the Holy Ghost making intercession!"

I will never forget, as a young believer, I was attending insurance school for a few weeks. I was sharing a room with a fellow student. Each morning and night he would kneel at his bedside and pray unashamedly. Over the next several days of school I was greatly influenced by his strong witness. His lifestyle seemed to be magnetic for Christ. I noticed that people were drawn as he shared the good news of the gospel with those who crossed his path. That week several were born again and I was also changed. That's the power of prayer and intercession. I haven't heard from this man since, but I still long to tell him,

"Hey man, Jesus found me and He has full ownership!"

While most turn to the world, the flesh or the devil, there are others who will cry out to God and will not be denied. He will come in, and flood their soul. The things they can't change, He can. So right now, make a move to Him, I promise you'll be glad you did.

Pray this prayer with me: *"Lord Jesus come into my life. Invade my surroundings; I renounce the devil and all my sin. Jesus I allow the Holy Spirit to take total control of my life, fill me and heal me in every way in Jesus' name. Amen."* My friend you have changed partners. You are now part of the family of God, so go and tell someone about your decision. Find a local church that teaches the entire Bible and grow in God.

Questions

Can be answered in a group, or as an individual

When you are saved, what does the Holy Spirit do for you?

Does the Holy Spirit bring you comfort? Do you depend on the Holy Spirit?

Do you think you can be a great person without the Holy Spirit?

What spiritual gifts has He given you? Do you sense the Holy Spirit daily?

Source Information

Chapter 1

1. 1 Corinthians 3:16NKJ

2. John 1:1-3 NKJ

3. II Corinthians 4:18NLT

4 Bishop Dale Bronner/ facebook.com(under his profile.)

5. Hebrews 11:13-14 NKJ

6. Smith Wigglesworth Devotional. Whitaker House 1030 Hunt Valley Circle, New Kensington, PA 15068 Compiled by Patricia Culbertson, 1999, May 16th, Pages 224-225.

7. The Word For You Today, Bob Gass, Friday, November 5th

8. Hebrews 11:35 The Message Bible

9. Hebrews 11:36-38 The Message Bible

10. Hebrews 11:39-40 The Message Bible

11. Psalm 103:20-21NIV

12. Hebrews 11:38 NLT

13. The Word For You Today, Bob Gass, Nov.13th, 2010

14. Hebrews 11:39-40 NLT

Chapter 2

1. The John G. Lake Sermons on Dominion… Edited by Gordon Lindsay, copyrighted 1949, Tenth Edition, Published by Christ for the Nations. Reprinted 1986, Page 26.

2. http://dictionary.reference.com/browse/committal

3. 2 Timothy 3:16-17 NKJ
4. The Message Bible, Publisher: Eugene H. Peterson, Ephesians 5:17-20 http://www.biblegateway.com/versions/Message-MSG-Bible/
5& 6. The John G. Lake Sermons on Dominion… Edited by Gordon Lindsay, copyrighted 1949, Tenth Edition, Published by Christ for the Nations. Reprinted 1986, both cites found on page 25.
7. James 5:16 NLT
8. Psalm 103:1-3NKJ
9. Mark 1:40-41 NKJ
10. Matthew 14:14 NKJ
11. James 5:16b Amplified Bible
12. Streams In The Desert, L.B. Cowman. Edited by James Reimann Updated Edition, July 10th, Pages 266-267
13. James 5:17-18 NLT

Chapter 3

1. Ephesians: 6:10-20 NKJ

2.Ephesians: 6: 13-14 NLT

3. Hebrews 11:6 KJ

4. Psalm 46:1 NKJ

5. 2 Corinthians 5:21 NKJ

6. 2 Corinthians 4:8-9 NLT

7.The Word For You Today, Bob Gass. Nov. 14th, 2010 "Take One More Step."

8. http://www.thevinetoday.com/word/archive/2010/12/10 Dec.10, 2010

9. Streams In The Deserts. L.B. Cowman, Edited by James Reimann. July 10th, Page 266-267

Chapter 4

1. Psalm 23:1 The Message Bible
2. Philippians 4:19 New King James

3. christnotes.org/commentary.php?
   com=mhc&b=19&c= Psalm 23, Matthew Henry's
   Concise Commentary online

4. Psalm 23:2b-3 The Message Bible

5. http://www.timesfreepress.com/news/2010/jan/30/
   Dont_quit_Keep_playing_lifes_music/

6. John 7:37-38 (Amplified Bible)

6. Psalm 23:3 (Amplified Bible)

7. Psalm 23:4 (Amplified Bible)

8. "WHAT SICKNESS CAN NOT DO." Dr. John Carr
   Even

9. Psalm 91:1 The Message Bible

10. Psalm 91:2-10 The Message Bible

11. Psalm 23:4b (Amplified Bible)

12. Psalm 23:5 The Message Bible

13. Psalm 23:6 (Amplified Bible)

14. The Macarthur Study Bible, NKJV, John
    MacArthur, Author and General Editor. Copyrighted
    1997 by word Publishing, a division of Thomas
    Nelson, Inc Page 762- Psalm 23:6.

Chapter 5

1. The Word For You Today, Bob Gass. Wednesday, 2/10/2010 "Jesus Stooped Down"

2. http://en.wikipedia.org/wiki/Compassion

3. Proverbs 4:23 NKJ

4. www.goodreads.com/author/quotes/ 2875209.T_E_Lawrence

5.JohnNewton,http://www.hyperhistory.net/apwh/bios/ b2newtonjohn.ht

6. 2 Chronicles 7:14 New King James

7. Luke 15:30 New King James

8. Luke 14:31-32 New King James

9. Doctor Archibald D. Hart, "Thrilled To Death" copyright 2007 Published in Nashville, TN, by Thomas Nelson. Page 3, What is ANHEDONIA?

10. The Best Of The Word For You Today, Copyright 2009 by Celebration Enterprises, Roswell, GA 30075 January 14 Amazing Grace.

Chapter 6

1. Isaiah 14:12-16a NKJ

2. http://www.lifechangingtruth.org/English/ArticlesEng/LeifJacobsen/TheAuthorityOfTheBeliever.htm

3. http://dictionary.reference.com/browse/authority

4. Romans 10:9-10 NKJ

5. http://www.jesuschristis.com/names_of_jesus.html

6. Luke 10:19 The Message Bible

7. Acts 19:13-16 NLT

8. Matthew 28:18-20 NKJ

9. Deuteronomy 28:1-8 NLT

Chapter 7

1. The Macarthur Study Bible NKJ, Copyright

2. 1997 by Word Publishing, a division of Thomas Nelson. Page 503, 1 Kings 17:1

3. Proverbs 3:5-6 NKJ

4. Psalm 68:1 NKJ

5. Haggai 2:8 NKJ

6. 1 Kings 17:2-4 NLT

7. 1 Kings 17:5 NKJ

8. Philippians 4:19 The Message Bible

9. Mark 12: 38-40 NKJ

10. Mark 12: 41-44 NLT

11. http://wiki.answers.com/Q/ Who_is_peter_ten_boom

12. The Names of God, http://ldolphin.org/Names.html

13. Hebrews 10:32 NKJ

Chapter 8

1. John 14:16 Amplified Bible

2. Acts 1:8 Amplified Bible

3. Acts 2:1-4 Amplified Bible

4. Luke 24:49 NKJ Bible

5. http://www.thestraitgate.org/devotionals/insights-from-bill-bright/testimonies-of-the-spirit-filled-life/
   Thursday, December 30, 2010

6. John 21:25 NKJ Bible

7. Bishop Dale C. Bronner, February 1, 2011
Facebook under profile.

Meet the Author

Howard A. Strickland is the senior pastor of Crane Eater Community Church in Calhoun Georgia. Strickland's passion is people; he enjoys watching the redemptive hand of a Mighty God at work.

Pastor Strickland has pastored three Churches, and enjoys working in God's kingdom everywhere he goes. As senior pastor the Lord has blessed his ministry with both numerical and Spiritual growth.

His greatest joy is his wife, Jenny, and they have two sons, Nathan and Daniel.

Howard's values were set into motion because of his faithful and loving parents, Charles and Barbara Strickland who are now celebrating 65 years of marriage.

Strickland has a Doctorate in Theology. He enjoys serving in any capacity through his denomination. He is active in the Gordon County ministerial association. He also serves as Captain chaplain for the Gordon County Sheriff's department.

He's a regular contributor to "Sermon Central" , the world largest online sermon resource center.

This is his second book as he enjoys helping others develop and grow.

It is his hope that this book will encourage and strengthen every believer. It will also challenge the reader to grow in their faith walk while believing for healing and miracles too.

Warning: The writings within these pages have been experienced, and could become contagious while bringing renewed fervor and faith to every reader that applies its truths.

For A Complete List Of Books By Howard A. Strickland
newpsalmpublishing.com or Amazon.com and your local bookstore

To CONTACT:

Howard A. Strickland

612 Shenandoah Drive

Calhoun, Ga 30701

For preaching engagements write or call:

706-263-3334

www.craneeater.com

For additional copies of this book, please make checks payable for $12.99 to "Howard A. Strickland" and send check to the address above.

Purchase at your local bookstore, or Amazon.com
Go to New Psalm publishing.com to print and publish your book today

Faith that Wins

A Book That Will Help You Fight and Win A Life of Faith.

Howard A. Strickland